POOL

a curriculum vitae

by
J. M. Tolcher

POOF © 2023 by J. M. Tolcher. All rights reserved. Printed in Australia. No part of this book may be used or reproduced in any manner whatsoever without written permission except in the case of brief quotations embodied in critical articles and reviews.

First Edition published 2023. Second Print 2023.

ISBN 978-0-646-87587-3

Cover photo by Johanna Ovelius.

It's Dripping font by Reema Chhabra.

For Jacob

Why don't you write the story of a young man, the son of a serf, made to submit to others' ideas, thankful for every crust and thrashed many times, just because he was a nonentity—write about how this young man squeezes the slave out of himself drop by drop and how one fine morning he wakes to find that the blood coursing through his veins is no longer the blood of a slave but that of a real human being.

—Anton Chekhov

I wished to postpone as long as possible, and to avoid, if it can be done, the moment when the barbarians from without and the slaves within will fall upon a world which they have been forced to respect from afar, or to serve from below, but the profits which are not for them... I doubt if all the philosophy in the world can succeed in suppressing slavery; it will, at most, change the name. I can well imagine forms of servitude worse than our own, because more insidious, whether they transform men into stupid, complacent machines, who believe themselves free just when they are most subjugated, or whether to the exclusion of leisure and pleasures essential to man they develop a passion for work as violent as the passion for war among barbarous races.

—Marguerite Yourcenar
Memoirs of Hadrian

POOF

[Enter DIONYSUS.]

DIONYSUS: Newly arrived in Brisbane,
I am Dionysus, son of Zeus, stitched up
    on repeat!
No matter.
Repeat your mistakes,
I repeat my lessons.
This world must learn, however
    reluctantly,
that it lacks the blessing of my rites.
I come to thrill you,
to make myself known,
now when you need me the most.
I shall thrash you just how you like it.
Take my rod without self-pity, my
    thyrsus of truth and frenzy,
for the time has come to unveil the
    story of the last of your gods,
that young boy shrouded in mystery.
Do you not think it strange
that the deified mortal,
he who was closest to your greatest
    emperor,
yet sits in darkness? It is no accident,
but rather purposely forbidden.
The deity's story is unknown because
his shrine is not for him at all: the
    sacrificial youth
in all his beauty has been used
as nothing but a shrine to Hadrian
    himself.

Look at what I possessed,
the emperor says,
*the most beautiful boy of all time belongs
to me!*
No longer.
Antinoöpolis has fallen like the city of
Ozymandias and
in the dust of this contrived sanctuary
the true story may emerge.
The false idol served Hadrian alone.
Are you ready to hear it?
Let me tell you of that very real boy
and the events that led to his
death.
Then, if you wish to pay him respects,
you may honour him directly;
not the emperor
who wielded youth and beauty for his
own gain.
Take to heart what I say:
don't be too sure that force is what
controls human affairs;
do you really think violence is the only
way to influence people?
You should reflect on this,
for even in performing the rites of
Bacchus
the receptive boy of virtue will not be
corrupted.
Merely he sacrifices himself
little by little
to nourish what seeds lay in turmoiled

                    soil,
          the scatterings of my vines.
          Why, here now come
          the women of the earth who have lost
                    their minds,
          turning in on themselves,
          resorting to attacking,
          of all things,
          femininity.
          O dear women! My sisterhood!
          Bang loud your drums so all may hear!

[Enter CHORUS of Bacchants, crazed women, led by JOANNE ROWLING.]

CHORUS: Oh, we can't believe we're here!
          Back again! Back again!
          To point out what's clear!
          You know it's true, and yet you torment
                    those in Dionysus' image;
          those hermaphrodites, those
                    gymnopédies, those damned
                    faggots too!
          The men flee with their fragile
                    masculinity.
          The women, oh, me too, me too,
                    me too,
          except now, yes, turn away as you
                    always do.
          Hypocrites, all of you.
          Here, a boy, basically a girl,
          shunned as both and neither,

will get raped and decimated and
nobody will care the wiser.
For our discomfort, he is to blame!
Little poof, burn him with flame!

DIONYSUS: I *am* a god and a
force to be reckoned with.
Men will twist and froth under the
    heavy weight of the stars.
Who better than I to induce the chaos
    and frenzy that will unveil the
    truth?—
your varying and frequently paradoxical
    desires.
Never before this world have I seen
such a backwards game at play.
Everything is true,
most of all the things that are not.
I do not judge you or any mortal
their shortcomings in being host to
    such an internal war,
nor do I feel pity.
Instead, I bring punishment.
Young Antinous,
smooth piglet,
burned by the flame,
must soon voyage home to the flooded
    city
and his tanned boys from Sunshine and
    Gold,
but the Bacchanalia has only just
    begun.

I empower him
while the Icarian Brotherhood denies
him. Here
he comes through
the darkness of the harborside,
all in white,
harboring darkness.
He is faggot.
He is poof.
He is freeballing.

    [Exit DIONYSUS and CHORUS.]

I

*The Town That Scapegoated the Boy Who Cried
Wolf in Sheep's Clothing*

I grew up in paradise. I will come to the details soon but all you must know is that home was a sanctuary. My parents made every effort to protect my sister and I from negative and bad forces in the world, to be role model members of society, and in this they perhaps succeeded too greatly. The result was my first steps taken outside this paradise as a youth were great missteps. I was unprepared for any conflict, believing the larger world, or at least my own people, to be on my side. Indeed, my parents denied the existence of any conflict, or their strategy for dealing with it was not to provide oxygen, thinking they could suffocate it out of existence. I also believed what I was told by them—that maturity, patience, peace, would serve me in the long run. As I reached adolescence, I began to understand the opposite: that I had been sheltered from conflict and viewed by my own people (amidst a variety of prejudices and despite exhibiting all their professed virtues) as a useless weakling. If I was to survive, I had to dismantle the components of conflict to understand them and to protect myself. By this point I was very much alone, a fawn with beauty and agility but little else to fight back against my own race. When I say I was alone I do not mean in physicality, but emotionally and spiritually. For example, on one occasion my father did tell me that if I ever got into a fight that I should punch the boy—I was never to fight girls—in the nose, bloodying it and sending him down instantly. This last resort for defending myself was also the only technique I was offered. How do I explain its uselessness? The boys were so antagonistic towards me from day one that I would be assaulted by them collectively should I go within their proximity. A one-on-one fight was unheard of, and I would essentially be inviting conflict should I approach them. I had been in a silent fight with my own species from the beginning but the sudden breaking of a nose would be so far from perceived as justified if I were to enact it out of thin air that I knew I would be the one to be punished. An even greater struggle was that I had never been around boys or brutality. It is one thing to slowly build up to war and bloody conflict, to grow up wrestling one another and learning those mechanisms innately, but it is another entirely to have a fawn from paradise to whom conflict is so alien be prepared and able to inflict this unnecessary pain. My father had only ever met with individual challengers, and he did not know how to advise me on a war in which I stood alone. He could not even recognise that reality. But I did not want to draw the blood of my opponents. I wanted to be their friend. In this battle toward peace I refused to admit defeat. I retreated from the world like a monk or philosopher. My unusual battle plan was this: 1) to know myself better than any other to prevent being wounded or shamed, 2) to know my opponents intimately to understand why they seek to hurt and control me, and 3) to look towards the furthest reaches of the stars to understand how I can best benefit humanity and finally prove that I am deserving of a place amongst my kind. To the extent any of this was conscious, I cannot say. Truly I was following my intuition and sensitivities, my primal desires, the very things I was supposed not to do, for if my parents had taught me anything it was to deny all darkness and exist only in light. Like Saint Genet, I was hot for the underworld, wanting more than anything to understand it, to explore it, though unlike him, my parents were alive and well and had not abandoned me, and I had a duty not to disappoint. Occasionally and guiltily I wished them dead so I could throw myself fully into the hands of terrible men and the adventures that came alongside. If that had happened I would probably be dead myself, or at least quite insane. I have them to thank for my life and probably for the telling of this story, for without them I may not have seen it worthy of our species to provide anything in return or indeed know what paradise looks like so that I could return to it. The underworld would have swallowed me whole and never let me go. Well, knowing myself as a fawn, I sought out the most brutal and powerful of men, hoping one would love and protect me. Instead, I found only abuse at their hands. I did not get what I wanted, but through the course of physical and emotional torture I learned the nature of those mechanisms of conflict that had so long evaded me. I believe I learned them well enough that in my thirtieth year I am finally capable of retaliation. Let this be my attempt.

Now, I must keep my nerve. I lost it twenty years ago (the timeline of my life I remember quite concretely, which is why I offer this story as memoir and not as fiction—let the truth be known—I am not of those writers that would diminish myself into subjectivity—these things *happened*) and I will not give it up again easily, as only through my absolute submission have I been freed from frenzy. On the night of the White Party, my very first Mardi Gras, I held this new power as I emerged from the shadows of the dockside tunnels to join the queue, standing in silence, alone in the drizzle amongst hundreds of intoxicated and screaming revelers. The loud groups of boys sandwiching me in front and behind must have noticed me on my own, but I knew better than to worry about their impression of me: whether something within me was fundamentally flawed, for example, since I was here without any friends. I remained centered, priding myself on a complete absence of the nerves that had overcome me for so long. Some girls cut in front, sidling by me and the boys who were too distracted with each other. Nobody tried to stop them, and I knew better than to bother evoking justice without an army. I waited patiently, eventually flashing security the ticket on my phone and letting them check my tiny bag for drugs. Nothing was in there but my wallet, which I had nowhere else to put because I was wearing only pocketless white football shorts, now mostly see-through because of the rain.

Once inside I did a quick lap and decided on one of the packed bars I thought I would get served at the fastest. I chose incorrectly. I watched as the flustered girl behind it avoided eye contact with anyone, barely coping and completely unable to keep track of her waiting patrons. A good half hour passed during which I noticed a man at the other end of the bar who had arrived before me become aggravated. He tried to be polite, waving, but could not get her attention—she refused to look up, to even survey the crowd. I could see his stifled rage as she served newcomer after newcomer in random order, taking forever to pour even a basic spirit and mixer. Spinning her invisible wheel of fortune she eventually chose the man next to me to serve. I thought of telling her, no, you need to serve that man at the other end of the bar, he's been waiting forever—but if I sent her away, she would probably never come back. To keep my nerve, I must not take responsibility for anything beyond myself: this will only lead to disaster. Also, I was thirsty (sometimes multiple motivations can be simultaneously true, and the presence of a selfish one does not mean the absence of a defensive or selfless one). Waiting for my moment to strike, I listened as the man next to me ordered two vodka Red Bulls before I interrupted—make it four and make them doubles. My shout, I said, turning to him. I did not want to wait here another hour. I did not want to be like that other man. I have been like him too often, in other situations, without opportunity to express my contempt at injustice done through the hands of the incompetently powerful. Not that I expected so much of a bartender. I have been like her too and understand the passionlessness of such a role. Instead, I have learned to take every opportunity to stay ahead lest I am knocked down by enemies or friends, who have over the years and in equal measure added up to little more than interchangeable crabs in a bucket.

A widely-known phenomenon occurs (and I will explain it here so as not to leave any reader behind) where, though a single crab in a fisherman's bucket may easily climb out, the consortium will not let any individual escape, undercutting each other, jealous of progress that they themselves have not yet made despite being capable of it, going so far as to even remove the pincers of a crab that insists on repeated escape attempts. In this way they collectively ensure their shared demise. I am not of this nature, but that may be because I am more aware of my own competencies. Believing myself capable of greatness I do not envy it in others, and I do not waste my time dragging down those that are succeeding. Knowing myself as somewhat of a target, however, I wait for my fellow crabs to focus their envy on another and I flee when their backs are turned, taking my freedom in the shadows. Some consider this to be Machiavellian in the worst sense of the word, but I'd argue instead that the general nature of our species is simple-minded and short-sighted, and I will not have my hands removed or wait around to perish because of our preference for competition to cooperation.

Escaping the crabs at the bar, I grabbed my drinks, finished one immediately and took the other to the balcony to watch the crowd. My new friend followed me.

"Thanks for the drinks," he said.

"I didn't want to wait."

He seemed nice, so I chatted a bit before saying goodbye. In this regard I have perhaps become guilty of the same prejudice that was inflicted upon me—my desires are provoked almost exclusively by men that seek to control or wound me. Romance has become tangled with conflict. I cannot yet tell you what I think or how I feel about this, except that pain and pleasure have both benefitted me in different ways.

I wanted some fresh air and went outside into the busy smoking area. Two men blocked my path, a handsome father and moon-faced son, adopted. We measured each other in silence until the father raised one hand up the leg of my football shorts, caressing my cock and balls. Moonface was quick to aggravate.

"You're boring," he spat, his jealousy as tangible as his father's lust, grabbing his other hand, the one that wasn't on my meat, and dragging him away.

Alone again, I whispered to myself words of power. I am kin of polarity,
>
> head and tail,
>
> seducer of the father and slayer of the son,
>
> then vice versa.
>
> The moon-faced satyr,
>
> hooves clomping, flees from my Shadow,
>
> Daddy in tow,
>
> rightly so,
>
> for I know what evil lurks in men's hearts.
>
> I'm hot, baby.
>
> *You're boring.*

A long time ago that would have bothered me. I would have wondered what was wrong with me to cause such spite. Now I am fueled by it. He was scared I would take his man. As they moved away the army of satyrs left no empty quarter, filled in behind his father who peered back and winked goodbye. I moved through this new crowd, hands replaced his, tracked their way up my leg. One of them I considered worth kissing, felt his cock in his jeans to make sure it was worth my time, then took him to a bathroom stall where I locked the door and pulled at his belt. I didn't have time to get it out.

"Give me your I.D. and your drugs!" banged some squalid demon that had found his way into disguise, insatiable to get his own. The satyr panicked while his hands fumbled to do back up his buckle. How these creatures fear one another. Sighing that I did not get to suck his cock, I opened the door and leaned against the frame, giving my new friend a moment to make himself presentable, and faced the demon.

"I'm sixteen," I said to the security guard, "I don't have I.D."

I cannot be undone. The lowly thief having then witnessed me as his superior thought better of his attempted robbery and escorted me safely off the premises.

On the street the satyr eyed me, concerned I had caught him in a trap.

"I'm thirty," I said, aware that the spirit of youth had not yet left me, though the legacy of which will abandon me if I am not to drown off a boat or crash in a terrible motorcycle accident. More likely it seems that I am to slowly wither in godforsaken New Farm (at least give me Venice or Amalfi) than to find my place amongst my Icarian brethren. How close I was. I bear the marks of death without death itself. No matter. I shrug off my own tragedy denied. Ascension awaits. (Either I am correct or must die believing so. Again, we will come to the details—but you must understand my journey first for you to understand my greatest lover/enemy.) The night had passed already. The club emptied itself onto us and we kissed in the rain, a transparent sea of white, our specters rising from the corporeal hair and flesh, and I lead him by his erection to his own bed where I had him unload in me, the power of my attraction resolute though upon return to our bodies, his blood not worthy of my fangs.

I patiently await my wild animal.

I am bled dry and must feast as the rich, of the rich.

I must reclaim my blood.

One of my fathers has taken it from me.

Not the first Michael who raised me, nor the second for who I crossed the world, nor the fourth, my pig, upon whom I experimented with the power bestowed to me, but the third whose sadistic attempts to destroy me awoke the power with which I seek vengeance. Maybe that is unhealthy, but anger is a powerful motivator, and frankly, I'm bored. I must do something with my time. The third Michael did tell me he wanted me to have fun, which is exactly how I feel about this next step in our dangerous game: let's see if he still feels that way once I've let loose. Anyway, the fault is mine. I mistook him for my Hadrian, for that great and brutal beast that would protect me. Maybe he will grow to be a better man, but for now I am disappointed in him, and even more so in myself. I did not know how such a mistake might hurt my pride. I have bowed to many men where, promised or unpromised, no allegiance was to be had, only the mistake of my total devotion where my service was not to be ended with the deed at hand but the discarding of my very worth, wisely so, for a slave freed will eventually return the pain inflicted upon him. The son will eventually kill the father unless he has been sufficiently broken. Those are the only two routes, harmony abject from this world, but I have stifled long enough. I gave my performance. Everything else was stolen from me.

I bring about my own restitutions.
I shall withhold no detail.

∴

"You're not allowed to play with the boys."

These are the first words I remember being spoken to me. I was four years old and had just started preschool, my first day at Vienna Woods State School. We had been split into groups, boys outside and girls inside, and as

I followed them out, I noticed one boy, smaller and darker than the rest, hiding alone in the alcove of the doors. I walked past him towards those many boys who, before I could step onto the playground, surrounded me in a pack. The biggest of them, Hayden, stepped forward to meet me.

"You're not allowed to play with the boys," he said, "you have to go inside and play with the girls."

I looked to the other boys nodding in agreement. Unsure of how to take on the entire male species that had collectively agreed I wasn't one of them, I returned inside as instructed. I started to play with the girls and the blocks, but the teachers yelled at me and shooed me back out.

I returned to the alcove, that place between worlds and the dark boy that hid there. His name was Ivan, and his skin was my femininity. We were friends until his family moved away, and then I was alone, just a little confused, but with an innate sense that I was not the problem.

The question arose: what the fuck was wrong with these people?

∴

I'll tell you what was wrong with them. They had been controlled by a dictator. Only years earlier a man, Joh Bjelke-Petersen, had ruled (though as with most dictatorships, the people didn't know they were under one, nor what freedoms they had displaced) and the distant capital of his throne had permeated the quiet shire of bushland and farms that was home to at least four generations of my ancestors.

The relevant details of their stories are as follows.

My grandmother Patricia wore a blue dress when she was married to my grandfather Ronald. She was pregnant and didn't think it was honest to wear white, symbolic of a purity that she had prematurely given away. Pat and Ron would raise two boys, the youngest being my father, Michael, born in the winter of 1965. However, around the time Ron was born, his mother, Ruby, had an affair, and we cannot say for certain whether we are truly descendants of the Tolcher or Strickland line, just that Mr. Tolcher did leave and James Strickland would become my great-grandfather and accidental namesake in first name only—accidental because my parents never thought of him when naming me, though they did not reveal this detail to him. I was always his favourite and James would hit me playfully with his walking stick, giving me silver coins in return. What's in a name? For once, a simple answer to William Shakespeare's query: in mine was a supposedly fun beating and an insubstantial reward.

Dad grew up on acreage, riding his motorbike to school and taking the ferry to nearby islands on weekends with little but a tent and some tinned food to keep him and his friends plenished on their adventures. Being the fastest sprinter, he was chosen to represent our shire in the capital and was surprised to find (though not without an ounce of pride), crouching at the starting line and glancing at his competitors left and right, that he was the only boy not wearing shoes. This story must have had some effect on me, because to this day I go barefoot where I can, occasionally walking through the city at lunchtime and enjoying the odd glances from strangers. Why would such a handsome and well-dressed boy not be wearing shoes? Why not simply conform? Why feel the cool concrete beneath his feet? And what if he steps on a syringe? All good questions, and to the last one I at least answer that I have remarkable vision and am quite capable of looking where I am going.

But for Dad, the grass and soil of the shire to which he was accustomed was quickly being paved over, the quietness of the bush destroyed by the shockwaves of territorial expansion now emanating from the capital, and new schools built with it. Dad became a founding student of a new public school where, because of his athleticism, easy demeanour and handsome charm, he was given the title of Captain for his entire adolescence. Meanwhile, by voyage from one end of the world to the other, my mother had arrived in this hostile place, her strangeness a precursor to mine own, the ignorant believing her homeland similar to the means of her arrival: Cheryl was outcast for having come from whales, living on their backs as an islander, or inside the belly of a great one. The traces were undeniable in her very voice, a disguised legacy I too would carry, for spiritual heirlooms differ from the physical in that they are identical in symptom but not in form. By this I mean to say that my lisp served the same function as my mother's Welsh accent. As Outsider, she would take her vengeance in claiming their Captain, he who secretly had nothing but pity for these people but was powerless as their figurehead. The stars had aligned in their unification all while the good dictator Bjelke-Petersen fell from grace, so that as they had their first child, a daughter named Amy, sodomy was simultaneously purged from the secular list of sins. By this time, as my parents purchased a block of land, the Redland Shire had transformed. No longer a distant rural community, it had become a far-flung outer suburb of Brisbane, and so, not on acreage surrounded by fields and trees, but in a home at the end of a cul-de-sac, they had a son named James, and though Joh had fallen and the laws changed to permit the existence of those such as I, it would be without embrace or acknowledgement. In such a vacuum and amidst an unrecognisable community, I was left to suffer, craving at least the punishment that all wished upon me but none would enact, for no action disallowed my reaction. I wanted to break someone's nose. With no choice left to me but to incite that invisible hatred, I began my long journey that I might fulfil the dictator's prophecy of my nature, to bring light to the silent war I was in.

The journey began that day, denied inclusion by my own people.

You're not allowed to play with the boys.

This rejection evoked in me a sense that I was, in a fundamental aspect that I could not place my finger on, different, and I sought to discover the nature of this mystery. The custom of my people, however, was not to share our wisdom amongst each other. Truth was wrapped in a shame that forbade any disclosure, so subtle in its effectiveness that any attempts to cross the threshold of silence was met with such incredulity that I could not bring myself to ask the very questions to which I most wanted answers. With this innate knowledge that I was different but unable to solicit further information, I immediately began stifling myself, convinced that it would be best for everyone if I simply pretended to be a normal creature. And what was normal for these children? *Normal.* As if the absurdity of life isn't the very thing that makes it compelling, and yet that absurdity brought them the most fear. No wonder I was about to cause a great amass of tears.

We would graduate through these circles of hell and told they were heaven, though they were in fact neither, for these people had seen to it that all magic was removed from this part of the world. What remained was the bleakest of suburbs, the very atmosphere so dried up and malnourished that I thought if I reached out and hit the air in just the right way, reality might crack and crumble into ash, but unlike the droughts covered daily on the television, and as I have repeated to you many times now, this one was shrouded in silence.

∴

We were placed into the care of a fiery woman with big bushy red hair, Mrs. Mora, who would spray us in the face with cold water on hot days. Vienna Woods, a poor public school, could not afford air-conditioning.

Mora had a penalty system and with it she would sow in me a single yet fertile seed of inferiority. A great canvas hung from the wall and on it, thirty pouches each filled with three coloured cards. If one of us misbehaved, she would remove a green card from our pouch, revealing a yellow card, followed then by a red card. If the red card was ever removed, we would be sent to the office, where I could not imagine any punishment as awful as the immense shame at having betrayed my own kind. Mora kept a daily log, and we were told that if we made it through the year without having so much as a green card removed, we would get a trophy. My eyes lit up. I had no doubts about my goodness and I would have my evidence.

But how would she attempt to keep justice in this chaotic class of thirty rats? (I merely call them what they would make me become next.) She could not. Instead, the slightest infraction would receive punishment, never mind what good intentions we may have had. Asking to borrow a pencil at an inopportune time meant losing a green card. Helping a friend with a math problem was synonymous with copying answers, which meant losing a green card. Any contrary assertions of the truth meant you were a liar, so you were penalised twice — straight to a red card. These rules were not told to us explicitly, but it was easy to learn from the mistakes of others.

I had again made a friend, this time a girl named Jax. With her I did not have to pretend to be anything different. We both performed the perfunctory tasks put to us at the top of our class. We understood each other. For at least half the year we were untouched by Mora's penalties.

"Pack up and get ready to go," Mora said to the class one day.

∴

"Time to get up," shouts the satyr, sudden and loud, meaning wake the fuck up, get the fuck out, but first come and kiss me here on the couch, I like how you look, how you take my cock deep and my loads deeper, (I look around his disheveled apartment as I straddle him—teacher's salary—not fit for my fangs at all), it was nice to meet you, now you can leave.

On the streets of Bronte I wish I had sunglasses. My head hurts. My white football shorts are more see-through in the daylight and I'm not sure if I'm grateful or disappointed that nobody is around. A taxi takes me to my friend Josh's terrace house, my phone buzzing from all the strangers that want my hole (I wouldn't need to remind you of my desirability except that this story is equally filled with scenes of my abjection, which creates a polarising existence—it is a wonder I don't have borderline personality disorder), and I fall into bed, alone, in the dark, getting up again when I remember to take my pre-exposure prophylaxis, and then back into bed where I drift off again. I need to rest. There's another party tonight.

∴

"Pack up and get ready to go."

Mora was taking us to the playground to fly paper airplanes, a simple activity barricaded by restrictions, for anything outdoors had the strict requirement of wearing a hat, and our hats had to be kept in our bags (or "ports", as Mora insisted on calling them). Our bags were kept outside on the "port-racks", which were completely out of bounds without permission, despite being no further than a few meters from the door. Following her instructions, we put our books and pencil cases in the trays beneath our desks and I watched as a small number of my peers began trickling outside to get their hats. Mora was with Jax, helping her with an equation, their backs turned to the door so that neither noticed the majority of the class now outside. A warning pang registered in my gut that we had not been given explicit permission to leave the room. I wondered if Mora had intended her statement to be preparatory, implying that we would soon be given permission to get our hats, though her phrasing had blurred that line. Indeed, most of the class was already outside, "getting ready to go", grabbing their hats as they believed they had been instructed to do. If she had not intended to give permission, certainly Mora would see how vague her instructions had been and how it may have been misconstrued, and certainly she would not punish the whole class. Even as she was now with her back turned, she must have heard the loud rabble outside and was ignoring it because her instructions had in fact been permission. I looked at her. I looked at the class. I ignored the pang in my gut and went to get my hat too.

As soon as I had walked outside, she became ferocious.

"What do you think you're all doing? Get back in here, now!"

Her face came to match the tinge of her hair as she unleashed her wrath, and I wanted to cry as she made her way around the canvas, watching her pasty white claws clutch at that which she had imbued with my goodness and now discarded, the shame so heavy on my conscience that it would not leave me for years. It didn't matter that I was good most of the time—this single incident became irrevocable proof that I wasn't good enough.

A few months passed, and on our last day of school, Mora handed Jax her trophy. Why did it hurt? As an outcast, proving my goodness was all I had. I would find a way to be like Dad, the Captain, so celebrated and adored.

Dad and I were not so different when we were free. Every Easter he would take us on camping trips to Girraween National Park, and if the nighttime sky was clear, we would use the light of the full moon to climb great granite mountains. I was only scared the first time, a little bit, but as a small child standing on the edge of perilous cliff-faces, my father's hand on my back and staring up at the cosmos that carried our world, I felt powerful. I sensed a shiver on my spine, a gaze hidden in that great darkness, something staring back. Around the fire, the stars glittering amongst the darkened leaves, I tried to concentrate on that gaze. I could feel it in the pit of my stomach as I turned my mind to ponder the workings of the universe. Strong like Dad, it was only when my nature was in the hands of other people was I anything else, anything less than masculine, anything incapable, anything bad.

∴

"You're only allowed one best friend, and girls can't be best friends with boys," said Catherine. I was surrounded again.

Friendship was a resource to be conquered, hoarded, and the girls wanted Jax. I didn't know what to say as Catherine took her from me. I was beginning to feel that I might be better off as a hermit in the woods if only I was allowed to leave this place. I pondered the whereabouts of Ivan. Had he found somewhere better? Or was it all like this?

Alone and from a great distance I watched the boys play, acting out strange monsters, a peculiar game of which I had no notion. Managing to have an aside with one of them (for none would talk to me under watch of the others) he offered me a bargain. I could join their games if I became his monster, a slave that obeyed his every command, and him my trainer. I accepted. He led me to the playground where the boys once again halted my approach.

"What's he doing here?" asked Jamie.

"He belongs to me and will do what I say," said Chris.

As they went through their list of monsters, the nature of my being was negotiated between them to be nothing more than a rat. I did not need them to recognize me as the desert dragon Scheherazade then, for only through this fate have I struggled to keep myself alive night after night: the greatest punishments often tied to the greatest pleasures and triumphs. As a rat and a slave I crawled through the dirt and cried strange noises for their pleasure, and this punishment was preferable to my suffocating in silence in that I might prove my strength, be it no matter that they would continue to operate in bad faith. After ten-thousand-and-one nights, I withhold no detail. Kill me, sue me, send me to prison for all I care, but out of respect for the dead, those involved, and those yet to live, no names or places have been changed and I have done my best to narrate all exactly as it occurred. That anyone has anything to hide is no fault of mine: I, for one, have nothing.

This is the truth. I will stand by it no matter the cost.

∴

Miss Jones, that pretty, kind woman.

She had organised a special celebration for Easter, each of us assigned a peer to whom we were to bring chocolates. Eagerly we awaited our gifts, those marvelous golden eggs and great bow-tied boxes. She told us that they were strictly not to be eaten until lunch, and then began to read our names. One by one, we each revealed ourselves.

The boys near me caught my attention as I heard their whispers.

"I don't want to give it to him," said Troy.

I eyed the half-empty sandwich bag full of tiny chocolate rabbits in his hands. Easily the worst gift on offer, as if to suggest that no deliberate effort had been made to begin with—but even that would not be enough.

When Jones called out my name, Troy didn't move. Nobody moved.

Jones checked her list.

"Troy, you have James, don't you?"

His face went red. He said nothing.

"Troy? Do you want to give James his chocolates?"

He started crying.

"My mum gave these to me! They're mine!" came his screaming outburst.

"Don't you think you should share your gift with James?"

"No! They're mine! My mum gave them to me!" he said, escalating into a full-blown tantrum.

Even the simple act of handing over a sandwich bag amidst these greater gifts was too much of a concession in acknowledging my existence. The embarrassment it would bring him to gift me anything in front of the class was too much to ask. We were both red: him with fury and I with shame.

"Just give him one," Jones begged, and he finally, reluctantly, pulled out a single unwrapped chocolate bunny and handed it to me.

He kept the rest of the bag, as well as a great big egg that was gifted to him.

I deserved nothing.

April was still a warm month in Brisbane and the tiny bunny, smaller than my thumb, started melting in my palm. Keeping my hand as open and as flat as I could, I tried to prevent my body heat from deteriorating it any further. The exchange ended and the class rejoiced over their gifts, the corners of my eyes stinging, skin flushing hot. Jones had been strict about nobody eating their chocolates and I choked on my words as I was forced to interrupt, to raise my other hand, draw attention to myself, and ask for permission to eat what was now nothing more than a puddle.

"Yes," she said.

I licked up the shit-puddle. The taste was immemorable. All I recall was the rage I felt, humiliation piled on top of humiliation.

I watched at lunch as everyone enjoyed their chocolates, my eyes red.

And then, on the way back to class, Jamie shoved me, hard.

"Get out of the way, poof," he said.

I didn't fall over. I wasn't any smaller than him, than any of the other boys really. I was perfectly average height (even a few centimeters above), though maybe a little slimmer than the others from healthy eating and physical exercise, riding my bike to school each day and camping trips. I didn't know how to fight, but I pushed him back and watched as his skin turned red, furious.

I ran, laughing.

I was the fastest runner in our class (like Dad), second fastest in our whole cohort, though where other boys were applauded for their athleticism, mine only made them hate me more.

He tried to chase me but by the time we were behind the building I already had a decent lead. I turned to him and smiled.

"Catch me if you can," I flirted, blowing a kiss.

He turned around and ran away.

At home I tried to tell my parents. I had been trying to tell them for years, to point to an issue that nobody else seemed to see except those children that wanted to hurt me. They reassured me that children were mean and that nothing was wrong with me.

"Something else is going on."

"No, no, no. You're a perfectly normal boy."

∴

Fuck, I need some caps. I woke up in a storm and remembered the fourth Michael: I had sucked him off in a cubicle by the pool area at the W Hotel in Bali while his boyfriend relaxed unsuspecting nearby. I scrolled through unsaved conversations and numbers, found him, sent a message; he had what I needed. I went to his apartment building where I met him in the basement carpark and made him my own, my muscle meth pig, forced him to puff, kicked him in his balls, his tongue black from the dirty floor, his own fault for allowing his seed to drip there (he doesn't ejaculate properly from the damage done to him but when abused he leaks), and I took the ecstasy I wanted from him as he quivered on the concrete.

That night, the satyrs were in harnesses and leather. I wore nothing but a green bandanna wrapped around one leg, my cock hanging loosely within, and a dog's mask to disguise me. A man took me home, tied me up, fucked me, kicked me out where I found a guy on the street, went back to his place and sucked him off. The sun was rising and I didn't want to find my way to the terrace house, didn't want to sleep. I wanted to be wanted.

∴

My neighbour was babysitting me. He was quite a few years older, a teenager already, fourteen or fifteen. We were watching TV and wrestling, his arms and legs wrapped around my arms and legs, my limbs splayed so I couldn't move, and then his hands squeezing my cock.

"Do you like that?" he asked.

If I answered, it was nothing more than a muttered yes. I didn't think I was supposed to like it, but I couldn't move, and it felt good. Something about being held against my will and it being done to me freed me from my own agency.

When I got home, I watched the gigantic wrestlers on TV and imagined them doing the same to me in all those various holds, throwing me around in some tight little shorts. When I went to bed I'd think up stories about aliens abducting me, probing me—always against my will.

I thought I had invented masturbation. I must have been the first person to discover it: why else was nobody talking about it?

∴

Mr. Buck could not control the class. Of all those assigned to protect us, he was the least capable and would break down into tantrums like my peers. It was during one of these tantrums that he decided to enforce a new seating plan. The desks had been organised in a strange formation of both rows and clusters, unlike any layout I had seen before. Four clusters of six desks were in each corner of the classroom, a long row of desks went across the back of the room, and, on their own, a tiny row of just two desks at the front and center. One by one he read out the names, sending the class to our various places, vindictively it seemed, for he knew who got along with whom and this was not that.

All I wanted was to sit in a corner, somewhere I could hide and be invisible, but instead I was placed at one of the two desks centerstage. I awaited the unveiling of my companion. The remaining options whittled away as Buck saved him for the very last.

Jamie.

He sat next to me quietly. I was surprised—no complaints, not even a groan? He hated me more than anyone. Apparently the emotions took a few moments to load and be released. Within seconds he started screaming. He launched into the greatest tantrum any of us had seen to date, surpassing even Troy and his chocolates. He cried and raged for what felt like a lifetime, demanding that he would not, *could not*, sit next to me. My shame was mixed with a kind of bemusement. I was the one being forced to sit next to this angry, aggressive boy that had already spent years bullying me: I should have been the one screaming. But instead, it was Jamie totally falling apart, losing all composure. What about me was so undesirable? I wondered if, sitting together, we might finally become friends and put this conflict behind us. Maybe Buck was smarter, more strategic than he let on—that this was his plan all along. Either way, if Jamie did not want to be my friend, his outburst would work to my advantage. If he would not treat me as a human he would certainly be punished, and maybe I would even be rewarded for handling this humiliation with maturity and be moved to a seat next to one of the girls that didn't find me abhorrent. I could see all the possible outcomes unfolding before me, and I was happy with any. I awaited my moment of victory.

Instead, Buck crumbled under the pressure of a screaming nine-year-old. Jamie was moved to a seat at the back of the class next to his friends. Another boy was ordered to the desk next to me.

"Why do I have to sit next to him?"

"Just do it."

I had thought we might be friends. Now, instead, I wanted to burn them all alive.

Only some weeks later I was playing chess with a girl and Buck witnessed my repeated wins. He made me play against him where, cutting into my lunch break, I won again and again before he gave up, beat into submission. I had no training in this regard. No playbooks, no teaching, no competitions, and no strategies except what I could invent myself.

Buck could not protect himself, and he could not protect me. The only deployment of effective strategy seemed to come from my attackers. If only I could have cried as sincerely as they appeared to—it would take me another twenty years to become that properly overburdened, and to write these words, screaming and shouting as I may as well be doing, going down desperado.

∴

We were eating dinner, Mum, Dad, Amy and I, and the television was on, something about the poverty line.

"We have less money than that," Dad said proudly, "these dole bludgers get it all handed to them."

"Are we poor?"

"No," he laughed.

"Are we rich then?"

"No… I'd say we are upper-middle class."

Upper-middle class.

Below the poverty line.

I understood he was proud of how little we had. We were comfortable, but that was because we never bought anything extravagant. Money was carefully budgeted. He wanted us to be content with the simple things. I believe this is called slave morality.

Then Amy and I were having an argument, over what I don't remember. All I remember is what I said to her.

"You're a poof."

She didn't have time to respond. Dad launched into his own tantrum.

"Don't use that word!" he screamed, "you don't know what that word means!"

Why was he so angry? I was amused and thought it funny to push him further.

"Well, she is a poof."

I can't remember what he said or if he spanked me (he probably did), I just remember the unhinged rage. That, and he never did explain what "poof" meant.

What was he scared of? Was it me?

(Can I also just mention that Dad's favourite movie was — and still is — *The Rocky Horror Picture Show*?)

∴

Another day, another party. I put on my little speedos and made my way to the Ivy pool where I ordered a margarita and found a chair in a corner somewhere to die. I watched the leagues of steroid demons in thongs and jockstraps dance, beautiful and sexy, and I wondered how they weren't dying like me. Maybe they're already dead. Maybe I need to die in order to properly join their leagues. Is that why it's been so painful to get here? Or is it that they just do G instead of binge drinking like I've been doing for the last three days? I made eye contact with someone familiar and it took a few seconds to click that it was the guy I sucked off that morning. We chat for the rest of the afternoon and he gave me some Ritalin which helped. We got a steak somewhere and he made a comment about it being a first date. I couldn't tell if he was making a joke. I couldn't stay awake much longer. I went back to the terrace house.

∴

I once again made friends with a boy. We shared the same birthday and started doing everything together—he even shaved his head to match mine (I hated hair getting in my eyes while I was prancing around). One weekend we were playing on his trampoline with water balloons that we pretended were our cocks, laughing as we wet each other, but on Monday he had Show & Tell and told the whole class about our antics. Whatever humour we had found in that moment failed to translate. As he laughed awkwardly and the class remained silent, I felt my face, as usual, turn bright red.

 He didn't tell them that afterwards as the sun was setting and a dusk wind set in, we sought to warm our wet young bodies by sharing a hot shower together, and that we thought it far funnier to piss on each other for real.

 His family moved away too, and I lost another friend.

∴

We were old enough to start playing sports against other schools, a mandatory event that again saw us divided into boys and girls. I avoided those sports where I knew I would be deliberately hurt by the other boys and ended up on the cricket team.

It was hot and sweaty in the sun, but I suppose that would have been less of an issue if I had been allowed to play the game. At home, Dad and I had played, sometimes with my uncles, and I never failed to smash the ball hard into the air—never failed to catch it as it plummeted out of the sky with the sun in my eyes. But we hadn't done any training at school and the assumption of our abilities was based entirely on our perceptible masculinity. Cran, the coach, placed me in a position way behind the wicketkeeper all on my own, the only boy on that part of the field. I stood for an hour waiting for something to happen. No ball came my way. No offer to switch places. Eventually I sat down on the grass, slowly burning in the sun, bored out of my mind and waiting for the game to end.

I discovered recently this position is called longstop. Longstop is hardly ever used. Twenty years later and I am still learning about the intricacies of how I have been outcast. Twenty years later and I am finding new reasons to be angry.

When we switched sides, Cran placed me last in line to bat. Just before it got to my turn, the game ended. I could have got sunburnt doing nothing at home, but I was forced to do it within vague proximity of everyone else, just close enough so I could learn my place.

∴

What do you do with rage? Do you deny it, try to ignore it? Or do you engage and try to fight it? Do you give up entirely? Well, it's not as easy as putting down a book and discarding a protagonist you do not want to embody. Suicide is illegal.

Shall I tell you about how other children were protected by their siblings, but that I was so contaminated, so toxic to social status, even my sister wanted nothing to do with me?

Shall I tell you about the time George, twice my size, violently knocked me down from behind in the middle of class, by surprise and unprovoked? Laying on the ground, staring up at this massive boy, I wondered, is this when I am supposed to get up and break his nose? I remember the sadistic glint in his eyes, knowing I was powerless, staring down at me as if to ask: *what are you going to do about it?* Assuming I could even get a fist in before he could block me, I had no visible injuries, and had been totally ignored by my peers. I could hear the questioning already: *well, how hard did he push you? That's no way to react.* And if I did manage to leave him bloodied on the ground, would they finally respect me? Or would they be waiting to ambush me on my bike ride home, to hurt me tenfold? Instead, I tried to get the attention of my teacher.

"Go join the circle!" she yelled over me. I couldn't get a word in. I stood there in a rage as the class continued.

And what of the long assemblies devoted to praising my tormentors for how well they played the sports I was not permitted to play, followed then by the long assemblies for only boys – that I was forced to attend despite apparently not being one – where I was punished alongside them for their destructive behaviour? Shall I tell you how day after day I stifled the pain from the sting of my invisibility, not wanting to bring any further destruction into the world, but was punished with those boys anyway, told that we were bad *without exception*?

I am not one of them, I wanted to scream.

I scream it now.

I shall tell you at least about one boy who appeared out of nowhere, walking beside me as I made my way home. He was a few years younger than me and had moved in at the end of my street. Early into our conversation he stopped me, staring at my hands.

"You're allowed to do that? My dad hits me if I do that. Only poofs do that."

I hadn't even known what a limp wrist was. This boy's dad might have hit him, but at least he told him what a poof was. Why hadn't Dad told me? But it was all starting to come together.

He kept coming to my house, breaking into our backyard to play with our dog, and I had to keep shooing him away, feeling guilty for sending him back to his abusive father and whatever other horrors awaited him.

Eventually he stopped turning up. I didn't have the space to babysit him. I had my own problems. The newest was having to check myself for mannerisms that might make someone think I was a poof, a Sisyphean task of trying to keep my wrists straight to hide what everyone had known about me all along.

I crumbled under the pressure of the impossible.

One day I went home sick with a stomach bug.

A few days later I was feeling better, but when the time to get ready for school came around, that intense pain in my gut came back, along with the diarrhea and vomiting. I couldn't get away from the toilet, and nobody had time to help me. Every morning Dad would be gone by six, driving off in his ute to be an electrician, and Mum would catch the seven-thirty bus to be a legal assistant. The morning rush did not permit any insight into my condition so for a few more days I was dismissed as sick and left to my own devices, curled up on the couch in pain until the morning passed and the sun was high in the sky and my symptoms all disappeared, strange even to me. By the second week of my discomfort, my parents were suspicious. They took me to see a doctor who said I had something called anxiety, and at eleven-years-old, I started seeing the first of many psychologists. At eleven-years-old, I lost the nerve that I had so far held against an entire community. They had succeeded in finally breaking me. Well done.

When they asked, I told them I was not bullied at school, believing I was able to stand up for myself. After all, did my peers not demonstrate their weakness to me daily, in their prejudice and in their tantrums?

I was the strong one.

I was not a victim.

And yet, here I was—paralysed.

And my successive psychologists were at an absolute loss as to why.

What a successfully camouflaged elephant. If they saw it, they were either medically, politically or legally restrained from pointing out my homosexuality.

All of it seemed to come back to this word: poof. At school, we weren't allowed to swear, but nobody ever censored us from calling each other poofs. Dad had been the only person to get upset about it that night at the dinner table, but even then, offered no explanation of why. Whether ignorance or negligence, the silence of the adults, the parents and teachers of my community, taught us one thing: that I was *less than* and that I deserved to be abused.

But I was a child, and I couldn't understand why I was so stressed—there seemed a disconnect between my strong mind and the anxiety that was overtaking my body. All I had to do was make my voice deeper, keep my wrists strong, find a girl I was attracted to. These were choices. Nobody told me what a poof was, but they told me what it *wasn't*. Everyone was given the same choice, right? The world was not hostile. I was just weak.

Every morning I would cry on the toilet as I shat my guts out.

"It's all in your head," Dad told me, "you just need to toughen up."

He said this with kindness, and incidentally it was the right advice, albeit missing a step. I did need to toughen up, to be myself against the forces that oppressed me—but what self was that? How many years now had my true nature been swept under the rug by all except those that sought to hurt me with it? With what armament could I come out skipping, limp wrists waving, lispy voice demanding to be heard? Yes, it was all in my head, but that was because nobody allowed the truth to exist in the real world. And after all, what did Mum and Dad know of the adversity I faced, the Captain who had been worshipped by all and the Outsider who mistook the abyssopelagic trench of my suffering to those known depths of her own? What great pressure I found down there, and in what darkness I began to hate myself, wanting to be all that my father was, but the unquenchable hatred within me growing hotter and demanding destruction, if not of my opposition then of myself.

I could no longer attend school with any regularity, and nobody seemed any closer to discovering the problem with me. I missed half of my final year of primary school.

Our class graduated from Vienna Woods and as always, most of the ceremony was spent awarding my abusers for their exceptional deeds to the community. Deepest Voice went to Hayden whose early impositions of masculinity would echo over the decades, Strongest Wrist was given to George for pushing over fags and pretending not to notice... I tuned out for the rest, faded away, disassociated into another world, somewhere where I didn't have to laud over them slapping each other's asses... and in that distant land, I could just make out an echo. My name was being called, somewhere far, far away... and then a hand grabbing my arm, shaking me.

"James! James!"

My consciousness came back into my body, the room coming back into focus. My parents were staring at me, shocked, saying my name.

"What?" I asked.

"You got Dux..."

"What?"

I looked around at the room, eyes staring.

"Go!"

I stood up from my chair, made my way onto stage. For a few brief seconds I felt as though I belonged. But then the ceremony ended and, as I went down to join my family, once again the boys approached me, blocking my path at the bottom of the stairs. I knew already they were not coming to congratulate me.

"You didn't deserve that," Jamie said, the others nodding.

I could see the violence in their eyes, the sheer resentment.

"Poof," they called as they walked away.

Vienna Woods would close its doors to me exactly as it opened them.

You can't play with the boys.

Any achievement I made only incensed them. My existence was an attack on the natural order and I was to be destroyed at all costs. How humiliating for all of them, being defeated by a poof.

And no matter how much I wanted to be like him, I would never be like my father.

On the way home, I couldn't contain my joy.

"It doesn't mean anything," said my sister.

My parents were proud but even they seemed wary of me getting a big head, as if my ego was the problem, and as if I didn't have to give myself so much love and praise just to match and counter the hate I was being confronted with. Humility was always the greatest virtue, though I can't help but feel it was one exaggerated by shame.

And if I was not to be treated as a man, not a boy, not even human, what was I?

Something that evoked chaos, frenzy and lust.

∴

One last party. A cute electrician kissed me and was surprised by my age. He ended the night crying on a lounge, his mistake thinking any of these people were on the same side. Yet how were we not, all those that had suffered identical exclusions? In a room amongst our own kind all the hatred we had for ourselves came to the surface, so that forgetting the targets that had for so long been painted on our own backs, we saw nothing but a room of red circles; the downtrodden attacking the downtrodden. In this way we serve only to fulfill one or another dictator's prophecy.

"See how the demons cannot control themselves! How they fuck and fight and steal, even from each other!" says Joh Bjelke-Petersen, say all the dictators of the world, denying us any inclusion or resources, forcing us to fight against fire with fire and then blaming us for our reaction.

Finally, home to Brisbane. My usual delight in an empty seat next to me reflected nothing but a numbness that had slowly overtaken my whole body. My previous lover had betrayed me, his secret consummations with another, and now I travelled alone. In the past I may have overextended myself to fulfill a false fantasy, but for once I held true to reality, not succumbing to the illusions that so quickly enrapture. I couldn't tell whether my heartbreak was the purest of all for its truth or the weakest for its inability to lead me astray, the question being whether the siren's call is a requisite of love. One man I allowed to destroy me entirely, the next to repair me, but neither of them held a place for me in their lives. What does this say about me? Self-awareness is a great hurdle, yet I refuse to be afraid, of all things, of myself. Now tell me: is it my ego that is delicate? I suspect the delicacy lies rather with those figureheads of power who fear to trespass against the status quo. I returned from my first Mardi Gras, alone, ecstasy and retaliation in my veins. I returned to my land for the first time wondering not how I might be perfect to another, only to myself.

[Enter DIONYSUS with the severed, talking head of PENTHEUS.]

DIONYSUS: It has been a while, old friend!

PENTHEUS: Fuck you.

DIONYSUS: Don't you recognise this room?

PENTHEUS: My old throne!

DIONYSUS: Yes, do you remember the conversation we had here?

PENTHEUS: It was so long ago. I remember you admitted to raping women.

DIONYSUS: That was not it. You asked about my rituals.

PENTHEUS: Yes, that's right, whether you perform your rituals by night or in the daytime.

DIONYSUS: And I told you by night, for the most part; that darkness confers sanctity.

PENTHEUS: As I said, trickery and corruption for women!

DIONYSUS: And as I said, corruption is found in

<blockquote>daylight too.</blockquote>

PENTHEUS: You are still annoying.

DIONYSUS: You are still superficial.

PENTHEUS: You still need a haircut.

DIONYSUS: Yes, that's exactly what you said next.

PENTHEUS: I'll cut off your love-locks myself, and those of your little fagboy, Antinous.

DIONYSUS: With what hands?

PENTHEUS: You both look ridiculous. That child needs further punishment to learn his lesson.

DIONYSUS: His hair is sacred. He doesn't know yet that he grows it for me. I brought you back here just so I could rub it in your face. Now fuck off.

[Exit the head of PENTHEUS thrown violently, followed by DIONYSUS.]

II

Finite Jest… Fear and Loathing in Alexandra Hills

"I'VE SEEN THESE MACHINES RIP SCALPS FROM HEADS," roared Mr. Bishop, the great oaf, "GIRLS NEED TO KEEP THEIR HAIR TIED UP TIGHT."

No mention of the boys for whom crew cuts were mandatory. I had, however, spent the spring growing out my hair, now a mop of dark curls.

We were standing in a tight huddle in the middle of the dusty Manual Arts shed where intimidating equipment, all painted an identical dark green, lined every steel wall. The rolling garage-style door was up but even that wasn't enough to keep the temperature down. It was the middle of summer. My uniform shirt was sticking to my back, soaked with sweat. Outside through the reflection of some classroom windows on a neighbouring building I could see the trees of the nearby bushland blowing in the wind. But in here, not even a breeze.

"YOU'LL BE PERMANENTLY INJURED, OR PREFERABLY, KILLED," Bishop continued, laughing, his tirade more a threat than a warning, making explicit the many ways we could look forward to our own dismemberment in his class, our bodies oozing as the sun reached its crescendo. I wanted the trees. The wind. Visible heat waves were rising off the pathways outside and I watched confused as the concrete turned from grey to blue. I felt my heart beating harder and faster in my chest.

Then, a galaxy of stars and fireworks crossed my vision, blueness flooding everything. I tried to stand still, to tough it out, and then I couldn't see, couldn't even breathe. I started pushing the other students, trying to walk towards that great open door, anything to get outside, to fresh air, to water.

"Sorry… I need…" I whispered.

"WHAT DO YOU THINK YOU'RE DOING?" came Bishop's angry roar, the last thing I heard as I veered off-course, blind, and crashed into the cold metal of one of the machines.

I woke up being wheeled into the sick room, though unfortunately for the staff at Alexandra Hills State High School who would have revelled in further reason to force their male students to have short hair, my scalp was still perfectly attached to the rest of my head.

I lay there in the darkness for an hour or two, listening as the receptionists outside spoke to my parents over the phone. I couldn't make out the words. I hoped they would come to get me. Eventually, one of the receptionists came in.

"You'll be fine to go back to class once you've rested a bit," she said, "your parents say you're fine, probably just dehydrated."

Well, I hadn't eaten breakfast. My mornings now consisted of uncontrollable panic attacks, shitting myself, unable to stomach anything without throwing up. Even water triggered my gag reflex.

"I can't go back," I said, "ask them to come get me."

She sighed and went back to her phone.

"They said they can't leave work. You have to go back to class, I'm afraid."

You're afraid? I was afraid. Everything kept getting worse, my body retaliating against me, and I couldn't understand why. Why couldn't anyone explain what was happening to me? Why wouldn't anyone talk to me? Why didn't anyone care?

Just dehydrated. Dehydration seemed more like a symptom than a cause.

"No, there's a problem," I cried, "my... anxiety."

It felt like an excuse. Some made up weakness in my head. But I didn't know how to connect my symptoms to their causes, to explain that I was dehydrated because my body was locked into a flight response, too traumatised from a decade of abuse to nourish itself, and that I was being abused because of a history of government policies and legislation that vilified people like me causing our systematic oppression (which had snowballed in the previous two decades due to the AIDS crisis, etc.). I mean, even writing it here, the whole thing sounds preposterous. And what would they say, had I, a twelve-year-old, managed to put together those words?

"Get over it" probably.

The result today is that I could care less about defamation: I have been defamed (defamation is defined as the act of communicating to a third-party false statements about a person that damages their reputation, such as "being a poof makes James bad and useless", but I guess it doesn't count when it's a nation-wide failure—this country certainly knows how to completely disenfranchise a well-intentioned young man) by all of you since day one, and if my retaliation in speaking up somehow makes me the culprit... well, as I've said, kill me or throw me in prison. I have nothing to take for nothing has been given to me, and if the obvious truth I am offering the world is of no interest, if I will not be defended, if the illusions of sociopathic dictators are preferable to reality, I will gladly die, or rot in a cell with other smelly men. I at least have my honour.

My body was insisting on its self-preservation, healthy boundaries: not to go near those people that only wanted to hurt and use me for their own self-interests. So began my teenage years, taught to deny my own security and safety, trained to believe it was I who was mentally unstable. All these years later I have no idea what I like and what I don't like. If I had been permitted to listen to my body, to remove myself and go somewhere safe where I would not be attacked, maybe today I might have a better sense of my own boundaries. As it is, I work daily to change my habitual desires to throw myself into self-destruction as I have been trained to do. What danger? It's all in my imagination, isn't it? Or is it real and I *owe* it to my people to destroy myself?

The receptionist, not knowing how to get rid of me, took me in to see the vice principal. Her appearance held something both callous and strict. I remember her eyes, dark as her hair which sat in a neat, short bob, the very face of law and order against the chaos. Sitting in her office, I tried to plead my case, to explain to Mrs. Jarman how I had been attacked and abused, but how I *wasn't* bullied, how I *wasn't* a victim—

"Your parents said you're fine," she interrupted, "just dehydrated. Drink more water. But you need a haircut. Get one by the end of the week or you'll be in detention every lunch time until you do."

Then she left to call my parents back, and to tell them that my hair had to be cut. I waited in her office for her to return. On the wall behind her desk hung a plaque, a quote by someone I'd never heard of. Someone called Hunter S. Thompson.

Life should not be a journey to the grave with the intention of arriving safely in a pretty and well preserved body, but rather to skid in broadside in a cloud of smoke, thoroughly used up, totally worn out, and loudly proclaiming, "Wow! What a ride!"

My hairs were bristling, a threatened animal in a corner, not sure where to bite. I couldn't believe what I was reading. She may as well have dropped a grand piano on my head thinking it was a music lesson. I mean, Thompson was the man who had shaved his head when running for sheriff just so he could publicly dismiss his Republican opponent with a crew-cut as being "long haired". I didn't know that at the time, but even as a twelve-year old this suckerpunch of words did not seem vaguely subtle, and yet, somehow, it was impossible to explain. Well, Thompson would commit suicide within a month of me reading this quote. Maybe news reached him of this woman's hypocrisy. Although, who knows, maybe she wasn't calling my parents back. Maybe she'd gone 'round the back of the building with a crack pipe, which somehow would have been more redeeming.

You have no idea what those words mean, I thought, spine tingling.

Nothing had been resolved. I suppose it was my fault, my inability to point to the issue which her entire staff were guilty of keeping quiet. Jarman returned (apparently sober) and sent me back to my classes, warning me again about my hair, as if this symptom of my abjection were the true root and cause of my suffering. How these hypocrites demanded my respect while offering me none. Any good humour I had was becoming increasingly finite. I began to crave power with which I could unleash a wrath upon them. A submachine gun would do, or a nuke.

Mum and Dad didn't want to make me get my hair cut. They tried arguing with the school, but it got them nowhere.

"You can't get everything you want," my uncle scolded me after my parents explained the situation.

"Yes, but I might as well try," I said, ignoring the fact that I didn't seem to be allowed anything I wanted, and that the reasons why seemed increasingly arbitrary. But the reasons weren't arbitrary, were they? Something very specific was being stamped out in me.

Why *did* I want long hair? Some small part may have been an expression of my femininity, and another small part may have been a rebellion, but mostly, I think, it was a display of authenticity. The humans I was surrounded by seemed so caught up in modifying their behaviour and appearances that the whole ordeal had become so stressful, so all-consuming, they had forgotten what it was to be human, to be a beast and an animal, and somehow, all the stress of this ordeal seemed to land on me who existed in the no man's land between the trenches of gender. Expected to conform one way or the other but finding it entirely impossible, it was as if I bore the brunt of our society's entire fixation on ego while simultaneously treated as if I understood it the least, a role of scapegoat I was not interested in playing. My long hair was an opt-out and a Dionysian allegiance to passion and emotion and the dissolution of the pointless, rigid rules my people seemed to place on themselves. I would lead by example, even if nobody followed me.

For fuck's sake, my hair wasn't even that long. It was barely covering my ears.

Jarman told my parents that I had no choice but to cut it and that I would keep receiving detentions until I did, so after school one day, Dad drove me to the shops, both of us angry and stressed. He didn't want to be controlled any more than I did. He had spent his teenage years with long, flowing hair, climbing trees, riding his motorbike around and never wearing shoes—all these things had made him Captain, and all these things were now against the rules. He hated the rigid conformity of suburban life that had overtaken the Redlands. We both did. In one generation, it had changed from a frontier of freedom and adventure to a prison of cowardice, no longer a place where the strong survived off the land, but a cheap outer suburb to which the weak retreated from the pressures of the city. And the weak had control, desperate to conform, desperate to teach us how to belong, how to thrive, how to be successful, a projection of their own failures. Why else had they fled all this way? What few remnants of freedom and personality I had were being taken. We were both powerless as the hairdresser cut my hair. I stared at my own face in the mirror, bright red, my armpits and my back drenched in sweat, my curls falling to the floor as I held back tears. I was twelve years old and I didn't know how to communicate any of this. All I knew was that apparently I was the problem, and my gut instinct that anything was wrong was apparently some intrinsic flaw within me.

As we left, walking through the middle of the crowded shopping center food court, I hated everyone and everything, especially Dad. I wanted him to feel the rage I felt and, remembering our conversation at the dinner table years earlier, I knew exactly how to do it.

"This haircut makes me look like a poof," I said to him, surrounded by strangers, quiet enough for only him to hear.

It worked. He couldn't yell this time. Not in the middle of the crowded shopping center. I watched his eyes bulge from his face, containing his fury as he stormed off ahead. I followed behind slowly, got in the car, and we drove home in silence. What a precipitous power my sexuality was.

∴

My parents didn't want to medicate me. They knew enough at least that, whatever struggle I was having against the universe, I would have to forge my own path through. Maybe they should have killed off the mental pain of not belonging and put me out of my misery, given me a lobotomy, but it would have also cemented the idea that I was too sensitive, that I was innately incorrect, that I had been right to stifle myself and that my anxiety was some irrational component to be dismembered from my body rather than a vital warning sign, my internal alarms going off, emergency, emergency, emergency. For isn't medicating and denying human sensitivity exactly what allows the dictators to prevail, drugging ourselves up on antidepressants and mood stabilisers just so we can be as sociopathic as they are? Is that really the kind of brutality to which we want to give power? Well, I am covered in the wounds of my battles, my physical and mental scars have hardened me, and with the strength gained I continue this retaliation.

My parents didn't medicate me for the same reason that I continued my education at another public school: they wanted my sister and I to understand how the *real world* worked. Dad was opposed to the inauthentic cushy connections and privileged mindset of private school students—he didn't want us to believe we were better than everyone, better than those from public schools. He wanted us to be down-to-earth and hardworking. Ironically, it was my experience in the *real world* that had burnt me out before I had even begun. In the violent *real world*, sensitivity counts for nothing. As I have said, value lies in brutality.

In the real world, it is normal to be assaulted daily.

Authority cares not for your plight and any kindness that does exist is so overburdened it does not have time for you.

All damage done to you is incommunicable.

Avenues to power are blocked by the status quo.

People will make themselves your opponents and they will wage war on you, but you will be to blame if you retaliate.

You will stare down the truth of humanity's primal brutality and suffer its thorns while you are told there is only the rose and that you are overreacting, too sensitive, and a girl.

You will be radicalised.

You have only known love and compassion as your guide, yet the unthinkable, unforgivable act of shooting up a school becomes all too reasonable and your best dreams are of nuclear explosions that erase all the anger and pain.

Elected world leaders and their communities disparage violence while dropping bombs, but the violence you feel at your rejection from your very own community, your isolation, and your daily suffering, will not be enough to validate feeling this way to anyone, for whether a bomb is an act of the aggressor or the reaction of the oppressed, it does not matter: if you validate the aggressor you are cruel and if you validate the victim you are a terrorist.

You understand why hatred is considered acceptable within certain contexts and though you have never been violent at heart, a Machiavellian approach may be the only way you will survive.

You understand that the real world is chaos and destruction but that is no way to live.

∴

My panic attacks were getting worse, not better. The next five years of my schooling life stretched out in front of me, an inescapable warzone, an abyss I was still descending into. One morning after my parents had left for work, Amy was becoming increasingly exasperated at my inability to leave the house. I had barely made it outside and was in fetal position on the lawn, clutching my stomach.

"Why are you doing this to everyone? Can't you see how much you're stressing us out?"

I ran back inside to shit my guts out for the tenth time that morning. I hadn't eaten and was dry retching on an empty stomach.

Stress often perpetuates stress. I was already mid-crisis and the extra knowledge that my sister blamed me—as if this were some deliberate act, as if I had any control at all, as if I was not caught in a cycle of reactionary emotions, a cycle that was now being made worse by being blamed for causing the stress that was preventing my family from operating normally, and as if I were the root of it all—was not helping. How could I explain something I did not yet understand? To tell her that my current state of being was no choice of my own but a symptom of the pain and prejudice that had been inflicted on me my whole life, but which I could not yet diagnose, for the ways I was tread upon were invisible in their systematic normalcy, and the reason for my being treated as such were as unmentionable as the truth of who I really was.

All I knew at the time was the problem was me, and if I could just toughen up, be more masculine, be a real man, everyone would be happy and the problems would go away.

"Why are you doing this?" Amy yelled.

"I don't know," I cried. "I don't know…"

∴

One tiny triangle of exposed muscular flesh is seared into my mind, two undone buttons of another student's shirt. Beyond them lay, barely exposed, the edges of his pectorals, just enough to see how the muscles had begun to tear, some small explosions transforming him from boy to man. I passed him on one of the undercover passageways between classes. He was walking with Jamie.

"See him?" Jamie said, pointing at me, loud enough to hear, "that's James, he's got a girl's voice."

His friend and I looked at each other. I noticed how those boys that got to play sports were becoming strong and beautiful. I wondered whether they could stomach their meals in the mornings, if that's why their muscles were growing so big while I stayed slim, and I noticed in my own body a response, an inner conflict: a clash between desire and anger. I lusted after the very boys that tortured me daily and had no idea how to reconcile those opposing emotions, had no idea how to escape my cravings for destruction their clash created. I tried to lie to myself, to convince myself I did not want them. I would spend the next years of my life making myself as small as possible, to avoid their attention, and in this, I was quite successful. I would avoid the locker rooms, the crowded areas at lunch, avoid any spotlight. I would be invisible.

∴

My second Manual Arts class was not in a shed, but a classroom. Lined up outside, Bishop ordered us to each sit behind a wooden graphics boards, one student to each board scattered around the room. As we went in, I hurried to a safe spot at the back and took my place directly behind one, but as the room filled up, two girls sat next to me. Two boards, three of us, one of the girls sandwiching in between.

"You have to sit behind a board," I told her, repeating Bishop's stern instructions.

As usual, they ignored me.

Once everyone had sat down, Bishop made his way around the classroom, stopping in front of me.

"I SAID ONE STUDENT TO EACH BOARD, ARE YOU STUPID?" he screamed into my face.

If he remembered me as the student that had fainted, he clearly felt no sympathy.

"I was—"[1]

"STOP PICKING YOUR NOSE AND MOVE."

The class was laughing.

"But—"

"SHUT UP AND MOVE. STOP WASTING EVERYONE'S TIME."

Only one board was left, in the front and centre of the class. The last place I wanted to be, forced to show my back to the whole class, feeling their whispers, my face bright red as usual, the corners of my eyes burning as I held back tears. I sat down exposed, my head and neck slouching lower and lower, my posture worsening as I tried to sink under the desk as they threw things at me. I wanted to die. And for the rest of semester, I would be stuck in close proximity to this screaming lunatic.

"I DON'T WANT ANY MORE IDIOTS IN MY CLASS. LISTEN WHEN I TELL YOU SOMETHING."

"Was he really picking his nose?" I heard someone snicker.

Of course I fucking wasn't.

∴

My name appeared on a list in the morning announcements one day. The Head of Department for Mathematics, Mrs. X (lucky for the old hag, I can't remember her name)

---

[1] In David Foster Wallace's *Brief Interviews with Hideous Men*, interview questions are replaced with the letter 'Q', though I like to entertain that this device is less of a stand-in for any questions actually asked and more an indicator of where a question could have been asked or a truth posited had the narrator been able to get a word in. If Bishop is not dead from some complication of his obesity I'd like to interview him, to really drill down into why he is/was the way he is/was, and by that I mean I would really like to just talk over him while I give my diagnosis, publishing a transcript with his responses as just "A". Maybe I could interview the whole Redlands this way.

had compiled our exam results and the top achievers were told that they must attend her classroom that day at lunch so that we could compete to be on her mathletes team. The notice also informed us that we were not required to join the team, but we *must* come see her to let her know. In hindsight this veiled threat of detention was more than likely a bluff and I should never have attended her request at all, but I still believed that doing what I was told would somehow benefit me, and that by fulfilling the duties put to me, I would eventually earn the respect I had been denied.

Like every other day, I hadn't been able to stomach breakfast, so by midday I was starving. I arrived at her classroom with a dozen other students, and as we were ushered in, a few of us attempted to advise her that we were not interested in joining. As she shut the door behind us, she drowned out our voices and told us that we were to take our seats and do the entry exam. She was forcing us, step by step, into doing what she wanted. She passed out the test papers and told us we had twenty minutes.

Half my lunch break, gone.

I sat there, stomach growling, watching the other students answering the questions as best they could, even the ones that hadn't wanted to be on the team. I did not even glance at the questions. I sat, arms folded, staring out the window. After ten minutes, Mrs. X said that anyone who had finished could come hand in their papers. I marched right up to her and handed over my empty sheet.

"You couldn't do *any* of these?" she asked, trying to work out how she had accidentally solicited an idiot into joining her coveted team.

"I don't want to join," I repeated, and this time she didn't talk over me. Her eyes narrowed as she realised who she was dealing with.

"You're *pathetic*," she spat, "Get out."

Her arm reached for the next paper in the queue.

I was free.

Forgettable bitch.

∴

I awaited my bridge into manhood, that important ritual, *the talk*, but it never came. Eventually, frustrated, I built up the courage and asked Dad if he would give it to me. Could he not see me becoming a man? Did he not care?

"Go to your room and I'll be there in a minute," he said.

I awaited him eagerly while he, probably surprised by my request, figured out what he was going to tell me. What secrets awaited, on love and life and darkness? I could not imagine. Eventually he came in and sat down.

"So, you're probably starting to find girls attractive?" he asked.

What was I supposed to say to the man who couldn't even stomach the word poof, let alone explain what it meant?

"Yes," I lied.

"Well, you already know how babies are made. You'll figure the rest out."

And that was it.

He left.

The discussions of love and sex at school had not taught me anything about myself. Mum, slightly more helpful, had bought a book on puberty and placed it on the bookshelf in case we had any superfluous questions, and when I was home alone, I would very delicately pull it off the shelf, opening it so the spine would not crease, so no one knew I had any interest in knowing at all. The expectation seemed to be that all of this information was either innate and instinctual or that we would uncover it via normal socialising, and that having to ask for it, vocalise it, teach it, was so awkward as to be completely out of the question. The only thing I seemed to be innately aware of was how embarrassing it was to solicit this information, even from a book on our own bookshelf. It also seems ironic to me that I was forced to study wood-working for two years and Italian for ten years but absolutely zero years on anything to do with sex or love or empathy or what it means to be human, which in my opinion are far more fundamental life skills and potentially linked to why everyone in the Redlands seemed so deeply unhappy.

I would pull this book off the shelf, making sure even my fingertips were free from any noticeable oil, freshly washed and dry, and I would look desperately for some reflection of myself, some information that would acknowledge my secret reality, and in there I found validation, not of myself, but of the trap I was in.

In there I found a single line addressing my reality.

Some people experience same-sex attraction, though this is usually a phase.

If I waited long enough, I would be normal, I thought. Whenever my parents left the house, I would rush to pull the book out and read that line, holding onto it, as if it was my life-raft in the storm rather than a part of the storm itself.

∴

The feminine counterpart to Manual Arts was Home Economics, everything to do with cooking and sewing and domesticity. Attitudes around male and female roles were changing (for only a few years earlier Manual Arts and Home Ec. had been gender segregated), but they hadn't yet changed enough. While it was now understood that girls were capable of woodwork and boys of cooking, gender was still seen as binary rather than a spectrum. I was terrified to step into either classroom, for that neat dichotomy was obviously not one I fit into, and the gendered nature on which those classes rested seemed only to serve in reflecting back my abjection.

One day in Home Ec., I had to go into the classroom next door to get water from the sink. Only one boy in my grade was out of the closet: Dean. We didn't share any classes but, on this occasion, visiting his classroom, he used the opportunity to come up and talk to me. As he introduced himself my face must have gone bright red. I attempted to avoid eye-contact, my heart racing. Why was the sink so slow? Water trickling out, barely filling up whatever saucepan I was using. This must have been what Jamie felt like, being made to sit next to me, or what Troy felt like when he was made to give me a chocolate. What would everyone say if they saw us together? I could hear their voices in my head, *the poofs are talking*.

I cannot remember what he said to me. I tried to be polite. Maybe I told him my name before I rushed out of the room, leaving as little evidence that we had anything in common as I could. I like to think I would have accepted him if I hadn't been so traumatised over who I was. But maybe not, for what fuelled the fear of those who had already hurt me? They could not have already developed the trauma that took me so long to stockpile. Do children innately hate that which is different, or is it learned? Either way, our community has a problem.

Back in my own class, I tried to sew as two of those popular sports boys came over and started playing with my hair. They gave me advice on how to condition it and what products I needed to use.

"You've got split ends," one of them said, mocking me.

∴

Leaving the school grounds by any means other than the main entrance at the end of the day was against the rules, but home was a direct route through the bushland behind the Manual Arts shed on the other side of campus. This way not only saved me ten minutes, but it allowed me to be nowhere near my jostling peers. These people might have been fine living like they had extra lives, plodding around hodge-podge with their contrived crew-cut hairstyles and silly uniforms, being mean to each other just for something to do, but I was busy. Busy processing. Busy healing. Busy escaping. Every minute I spent amongst them caused me damage, and I needed every minute I could to myself. On one of these afternoon escapes, I was doing a double-whammy. Not only was I leaving via a non-exit, I was leaving in my sports uniform. Just as I was about to pass the last building, a teacher I didn't know walked around the corner, right in front of me.

"Well, think you're better than everyone else, do you?"

Now *that* was a complex question. The variables were immense.

Let's start with the uniform. Three days a week I had to get changed for Physical Education, and then get changed back. Getting changed in the locker room was, quite simply, suicide, and the only thing worse than going in there and getting attacked would be going in there and getting an erection. The alternative was to get changed in a quiet bathroom somewhere, which presented an entirely new set of issues. If you have not been into a men's public bathroom, especially one frequented by teenagers, visiting one would make you believe that the purpose of the location is not to relieve the body of urine but rather to mark one's territory as vigorously and messily as possible. It was as if they knew the poofs had nowhere else to change and deliberately did all they could to make it uncomfortable. The whole process was fraught with danger. I had one or two bathrooms I preferred, ones that were tucked away and not frequently used. If a boy was in there, I would usually go back out, stand somewhere nearby, wait for him to leave, and go back in. Now this next part had to happen quickly: who knows who might come in and find me trapped in a corner, naked. (Whoever designs men's bathrooms seems to have the terrible habit of offering copious urinals and only ever one or two cubicles, which is to say that it's not my ideal location to shit or get changed either, but for a homosexual boy with anxiety, I have often had no choice in either matter, and the lack of clean and secure options feels targeted and spiteful, salt in the wound.) Walking in, I would inspect the stalls, picking the cleanest one I could. Rarely was there a *clean* option, but rather a choice between a toilet blocked with shit and paper or a stall where someone had pissed up the wall. The safe option here might not be what you would expect: the disgusting shit-blocked toilet was preferable. I needed dry land to put my bag on (on top of the toilet, the only surface, was not an option) and this meant piss-soaked floors were the biggest hurdle. These bathrooms were a minefield of piss-puddles. Now, assuming there was a stall with at least a patch of dry floor, I would lock myself in, put my bag down, put the toilet seat down, and use copious amounts of single-ply to dry off the similarly soaked lid, doing my best not to get my finger's damp. Then, sitting down on the toilet, I would carefully remove one shoe and one sock at a time to prevent putting my foot down and having my sock wet with urine for the rest of the day. If my bare feet stepped in piss, that could be dried, but a wet sock meant I was done for. I would be cursed to feel that groggy, damp mess in my shoe for the rest of the day, bacteria spreading… The next part was slightly easier, but still required precision. Stripping off my uniform, I would fold and balance it neatly on the toilet seat, careful not to let anything fall onto the ground. Then, pulling my sport uniform from my bag, I got dressed, replaced my normal uniform into my bag, sat back on the toilet, dried my feet with toilet paper, and put on my other shoes. If this entire juggling act was done quickly enough, nobody else would walk in, and I could leave with my chin up. If not, the gaps under the stall were large enough that anyone could see I was too pussy to get changed in the locker room, and if I was not subject to outright ridicule, I knew at least what they would be thinking. The worst situation was when every bathroom stall was filthy to the point of being unusable and I was forced to change frantically in a dry corner, terrified of being caught in the open.

All while the "normal" boys changed in clean conditions. That I felt it unfair to subject myself to this change-of-uniform routine, not once, but twice, just to walk five minutes around the corner to my home and get changed again, all for the purpose of giving this bottom-of-the-barrel school the most hollow presentation of civility on that short walk, as if any of the meth-heads peering out of their crack-den windows cared, seemed to me entirely justified, and had little to do with any feeling of superiority I may have been carrying. The whole thing was too exhausting, too shameful, to make me think I was better. It was only a small preservation of what little ego and little pride I had left. With regard to the *practicality* of getting changed, no, I did not think I was better than everyone else—it seemed, in fact, proof to the contrary. With regard to the *superficiality* with which my presentability was used to promote a false idea of the school's civility—well, yes, seeing through this ruse and not wanting to participate in it did give me a sense of superiority.

The route I chose to take home presented a similar set of variables. The urgency with which I needed my own time in order to process my pain seemed to me to be pivotal, vital information for the human race (clearly I was not the only unhappy soul in Alexandra Hills, though I might have been the only one wondering why, or indeed how to improve things) and the absence of anyone else that seemed to care made me think I might be "better" as well.

But who did he mean by *everyone else*? That was a large category. If he was referring to the people that used their power to marginalise others for their own gain or the people that passively accepted this happening because they had no moral backbone or lacked the intelligence to think about it, then the answer was yes, obviously, to both. Why should I have to parade around in these putrid clothes detouring via an unnecessarily specific exit when all I was offered in exchange was abuse?

But then, noting the delusions that seemed to enrapture not just my peers but the adults and leaders of this world, how could I be so sure I was not suffering from some similar crisis, totally invisible to myself? How could I be convinced of my superiority when everyone else seemed so mistakenly convinced of theirs? The whole thing was a mindfuck.

Finally, what does *think you're better* even mean? The question seemed to impose that hierarchies of any kind were bad even though this teacher in this very moment was exerting his will, believing himself "better" and worthy of punishing me, and therefore an entirely hypocritical question to be positing in the first place. Frustrating when my goal in establishing my place in the human hierarchy was not for the primary purposes of either sadism or ego but actually to help these lost and confused people, to teach them that they did not have to live within the confines of the prison they had built for themselves, but indeed could leave it via any route and wearing whatever clothes benefitted them the greatest without any damage to anyone.

Also, I was twelve-years-old, and these thoughts were largely an untranslatable gut feeling, something I knew was true but not sure how to put into language.

"No," I muttered quietly, at the very least aware of the answer that was going to free me from this situation sooner rather than later.

"Get changed and come meet me at the assembly hall."

So began the whole delicate process again, finding a stall free from piss, carefully keeping my socks dry, the long walk back across campus, keeping my eyes on the floor while this ugly man berated me, told me I needed a haircut, and then the long walk back towards my home. I peered over my shoulder carefully as I left the hall, making sure he wasn't watching me, following me. I would not go through the front entrance. I made my escape, not in the uniform I wanted, but out the back exit through the bush. I would not follow their rules. I would have my freedom.

∴

Mum told me she was worried I was going to kill myself. No, I would tell her, how could I do that to you? She was right though. I wanted to die. My anxiety had bled into depression, hand-in-hand as those two often go, and I no longer wanted anything for myself. At thirteen years old, I dreamed of death and annihilation. Even as a boy in my class told me that he and a few others would be going to the gym after school to build muscle, I could not admit to myself the thing I really wanted.

"You should go too," he said, "what if you get into a fight?"

Well, I was frequently assaulted, always in small, surprising and witnessless ways, but I could not imagine ever lowering myself into that arena on purpose. Not that I was not capable of violence: I craved it more than anything else, but I did not want to bring further mayhem into the world. Out of touch with myself as I was quickly becoming, this internal battle of emotional repression, instinct against reason, saw me lost and confused. I knew at least that physical violence was not my territory, not my strength, and I failed to see how going to the gym and fending off a few hounds would reverse the tide of whatever greater malignity I had gained sense of. I looked passed my opponents of the day, too sympathetic of their plight and weakness, those students and teachers who understood so little, submissive dogs to my true grievance which seemed to lay elsewhere, if only I could pinpoint my suffering. With no roadmap, I was hungry for only some cartography in this darkness.

"Why would I get into a fight?" I laughed.

"Sometimes fights just happen."

I suppose he was right, for I was already in one—but there would be no winning through physical brawl. Any interest I had in attending a gym was as opposite to violence as possible. I had noticed the bulging muscles on many of the athletic boys and would have liked to work out myself if only to further my desirability (for when I looked in the mirror I knew that I possessed the trait despite the protestations of my peers), but to admit this was too close an admission of my sexuality, a truth I was still fleeing from. How many of these boys were operating under the guise of violence to become more attractive to their quarry, masculine or feminine? And why was violence the acceptable motive, not love? I did not want to be violent despite the growing anger inside me, and the passive contributions exercise had to health and fitness were of little interest to me: I wanted to be beautiful and was too ashamed to admit it. The place I most wanted to be was being suggested in this very moment and yet I could not attend it, for I could not admit my nature amidst a people so contrary to myself—I required the knowledge with which to first build a foundation for myself to stand on, the recipes and instructions to which were being hidden from me, but a secret library that I would access through intuition, knowing not what I sought, only that I would certainly recognise it upon its apparition. What a sad people who could not have beauty without the excuse of violence—with all my creativity I sought a bypass, and I was met with a miracle.

One day, Dad came home and told us of news he had heard on the radio. Two new public schools were opening for the best and the brightest students in the state: the Queensland Academies for Science, Maths and Technology, and for Creative Industries. My sister and I applied, though my parents were surprised when I insisted on Creative Industries. I had always excelled in my studies and they assumed I would want to follow a more traditional route. I did not know how to explain to them that I saw myself as an artist and a romantic; certainly, nobody saw me that way. But following a process of interviews and entry exams, we were accepted. A lucky and last-minute escape.

On my last day at Alexandra Hills, Jarman approached me. Her eyes, as usual, had acquired their target.

"Your hair is too long! You need to get it cut or you'll be in detention every day—" (the usual diatribe).

Before I could say anything, a girl I knew, a friend, Madi, jumped in to defend me.

"It's his last day," she said, with a satisfying what-are-you-going-to-do-about-it attitude.

Jarman glared at the both of us.

"And where are you going?"

Technically we still had two weeks of classes, so she mustn't have liked the idea of my early vacationing.

"He got into the Queensland Academy for Creative Industries," she said, again delivering it with all the self-righteous pompousness it deserved.

Jarman's mood suddenly changed from gruelling contempt to starry-eyed praise.

"Oh! Congratulations! I thought none of our students got in!"

"Yeah," I said, "I'm allowed to have long hair there."

"That's wonderful," she beamed, "well done!"

My words were as lost on her as the ones on the plaque on her wall. It was Thompson too who said in a world of thieves, the only final sin is stupidity.

And that night, at home, an instant message came through on my laptop.

"Your life won't be any different," one of the crabs said, claws furiously snipping as I disappeared over the lip of the bucket.

∴

Anxiety-provoked diarrhea is even worse when you have to catch a bus to school. Previously, the short walk up the street had meant I was never far from a toilet, but we had moved to Stafford on the other side of the city and the same short walk barely got me to the bus stop. From there, the bus would crawl on a journey that would take at a bare minimum the better part of an hour through peak traffic, creating an existential purgatory in which I could do nothing but sit with my increasing levels of panic, occasionally getting off at random stops to rush to find a public bathroom in a park or shopping complex before I shat myself.

Waking up was my worst nightmare. I knew the anxiety was inevitable. I would go to sleep hoping that I would die in the night so that I would not have to suffer another day of being myself, but every day I woke up in despair. Mum started bringing me coffees and Berocca drinks in the mornings, wondering why I had no energy, but I would fall back asleep drink in hand, spilling it all over myself and my sheets. Our best efforts weren't working and eventually she stopped trying. It's not hard to figure out why I had no energy. I had nothing worthwhile to invest it into. The emotional truths of my life were so stifled, getting out of bed was pointless. I wanted to die.

But the Academy saved my life. I was far closer to my tribe (though our reality still went largely unmentioned and entirely untaught), and a few of my peers were even out of the closet. Ninety-percent of the student population was female, so I was safe from any further harassment. But the damage had already been done. I came to the Academy with an ego in tatters, an anxiety disorder that still made it impossible to face up to each day, and while it offered me a safe place to heal, I wasn't exactly fit to make the most of the opportunity that finally presented itself to me. I should have been thriving, but I couldn't even get out of bed. I was not motivated for anything. The Redlands—the Deadlands—had destroyed me completely.

The teachers at the Academy were for the most part geniuses (and very kind, to the point where I can't recall any unprovoked abuse from them at all). In one business class, on the topic of advertising, our teacher suggested we think of products that are marketed to us, that we see on the morning television for example, and that evoke in us a desire for consumption. I raised my hand, confused.

"What if we don't ever want to buy anything?"

She didn't know how to respond.

"You don't want anything? There is nothing in the world you want to purchase?"

And it was the truth. By age fifteen, I was so cut off from my desires, so deep in my depression, there was nothing I craved except death itself. I stared into the world of materialism and felt nothing.

But that desire did eventually rise elsewhere.

Confronted at so early an age with the certainty of death and no chance of my own pleasure, combined with the culmination of my senior schooling years in which I was expected to know how I might make myself useful to my people, the question arose: how do I put my death to good use? Another ten years of displeasure in studying medicine so that I might finally assist a community of people that did everything in their power to make me sick? Or slightly less in studying law so that I might deceive and manipulate them?—it was clear to me that Justice had long been absent. Both would supply me the perception of being a necessary and good contributor to Australia, though I understood already those highly paid benefactors serve entirely with the selfish knowledge of their reward and their standing. No, surely with this courage I had found (for courage I had found through the process of these trials and considerations) I could become something more than those confined to playing such simple roles as lawyer and doctor. I shall play the all-or-nothing game, I thought, Madman-or-Saint, for I the unbeliever have the greatest faith of all! Do you not see how the believers give up their faith for something to believe in? Faith lies in chaos alone. In that truth, in my frenzy of anxiety against death and the unknown, I found desire. I tried but could not manage to explain this to anyone, and so, in solitary, I began my journey, and found that by following this desire I was able to meet the gaze of the abyss directly. In this way I began to overcome the anxiety that had now controlled me for the greater part of a decade, for staring into the inevitability of my own death, I no longer feared the petty and irrelevant tribulations of day-to-day life and the simple creatures that lived there (consciously, anyway—my nerves were still shot and there was little I could do to repair the damage done to my physical and unconscious systems). The process was slow and the work was difficult, wading through the sludge of darkness alone, but it was a direction, even if I could not explain it to my stressed teachers and career counsellors who did not understand why this bright young man on the cusp of the world was imploding. Their job was to address my next step into the light—but they could not see how far away that light was, and how much darkness still lay before me. After all, I was making the journey without so much as a torch.

I was the only person I knew that would catch the morning bus to school thinking of nothing but my own death to quell the fear and hatred inside, the most absurd of balancing acts where my anxiety and depression were simultaneously hand-in-hand, fueling each other while acting as each other's counter, an internal battle of star-crossed lovers. Deep in a state of panic, I would balm myself with a deliberate existential crisis, and as my anxiety shrunk, my depression grew greater and greater, overcoming me completely. The cure to my fear, my pain and my suffering, was to embrace that everything—my life especially—was meaningless.

As I have said, the Academy was a place of acceptance, but I had arrived at this haven too late, the damage already done. I was frantic, the disturbed surface of my being reflecting those tumultuous depths. Here I was not ostracised so much as dismissed as weak for my broken ego, which further frustrated me. I carried the burden of conflict within our entire community, saw the silent truth, and yet the damage done to me was considered a symptom of my weakness rather than my strength despite everyone else's inability to carry it. I remained, as a result, largely alone. I did make an acquaintance with one boy, Tom, and for a little while we made our attempt at male bonding. Tom was animated and intelligent, but I suspect similarly affected by the expectations of fulfilling a male persona, as despite his intelligence, he seemed to embrace an ego of stupidity, stifling his mind in the same way I stifled my feelings. Tom would eat half-a-dozen eggs for breakfast, a whole chicken for lunch, and was constantly working out. I watched as his body became more muscular, biceps and abdominals rippling under his tight skin. His affectation of the dumb muscle jock persona made perfect sense, though none of this, to my knowledge, was an attempt at covering up sexuality—just, it seemed, a way of smoothing off his rough edges to become the easily digestible male that everyone loved. I say this without judgement as I was just as affected, with my long hair and skinny frame, both of us fighting against ourselves, confused and trying to fulfill some strange expectations we did not understand. If anything, he understood the assignment better than I did, or at least was better able at fulfilling the male criteria. My reaction was to reject criteria in its entirety.

    I was deliberately confronting my anxiety, working through it, and managed to sleep over at Tom's place once or twice. His father, Mr. Allen, a successful barrister, picked us up from school one day. He stared me down in the car. My hair at this point was halfway down my back.

"Principal Jose lets you have that hair, does he?" he said, disapprovingly.

"Yes," I said. Out of all the things in the world to be upset about, why was my hair always top of the list?

I felt hurt. We had been reading *To Kill A Mockingbird* and I had admired Atticus Finch for being able to see through social prejudice, but Tom's father didn't see my struggle, he just saw the symptom and decided it was the problem. No one wanted to stop the cause of my suffering, but everyone wanted to stop me from having long hair. I thought successful men of the law were supposed to know good from bad. All this one knew how to do was follow rules, and if Mr. Allen had been in Atticus' place, I can only assume he would have skinned Tom Robinson to fix the problem. Well, I was sick of the rules. I was sick of being controlled. I didn't hang out at Tom's place after that. And I couldn't imagine why anyone in their right mind would want to study law.

I tried to explain these thoughts to my parents, teachers, psychologists, guidance counsellors, to no use. No one ever seemed to have any answers or know what to do with me, but the consensus seemed to be that I was the one who didn't understand. Indeed, it felt like I was missing some vital piece of information.

"One day you will understand how the real world works," I would hear, over and over again, as if the problem of assimilation lay with me.

The real world. How I have come to despise those words, as if the contrivances of man in those billions of neat filing cabinets documenting rape in its legal form could surmise it. What a labyrinth we have built for ourselves, from the periphery of which I peer in, a bird's eye, my Shadow can be seen on the walls, a conspicuous hint of the true reality denied. I am alone amongst these men, they who enter the labyrinth with the promise of greatness as lawyers and doctors and accountants and politicians, they who will never see the truth of the world for they cannot digest it. The abyss assaults them and they cannot meet its gaze. How many years have I now stared into it? I have felt its own trepidation rising again and again like a shiver up the spine of the world since I awoke here. Indeed, I only met its gaze for my own people would not look me in the eye and I was forced to journey to the source myself. In these great men I see nothing but cowards, those who knock me down in darkness.

    I shall make my massacre public. Let us have this battle in the light. Exile me to France, but to this day whose name do we remember? The corrupt lawmen that sent him away, or Oscar Wilde?

∴

Just before beginning my senior year, student elections were held to decide on our School Captains. One of the Captains from my sister's cohort, Alex, came to give us advice on our applications. I listened as he made his way patiently around a handful of my peers, offering them helpful suggestions and improvements. Leaving me for last, he offered me one short question.

    "Do you really think you're cut out for this?"

    Shaking his head and without waiting for an answer, he walked away.

It was no mystery to me why he said that. My damaged, fragile ego, my long hair, my flamboyancy, all added together to give off a solid impression of incapacity. The problem was that I knew too well what I was capable of but had no idea how to come about a resolution, to reconstruct myself in a way where people would take me seriously. I remembered the confidence and self-assurance I had in the years prior to my anxiety disorder, and I wondered how to get back to being that person and assimilate properly into the social order. I refused to take the place that had been given to me at the bottom. I would not succumb to that prejudice. But prejudice was the gatekeeper of ego, ego was the requirement of assimilation, and ego was what I had been denied from the very beginning. I would never be able to fulfill my potential and my capacity without one.

The elections were held and, of course, I lost.

An intelligent girl I got along with named Rebecca was given one of the positions, and with her I tried to raise some of these issues, to discuss the nihilism I was being overcome with and to delve into the kinds of philosophical questions that were plaguing me. Nihilism is the belief that life is meaningless, and, taught that I was supposed to ignore my constant beatdowns and humiliations, ignore my own feelings and emotions, never speak up for myself, how could I have believed in anything else? If the worst things that happened to me meant nothing, if my achievements meant nothing, suddenly everything felt silly and laughable. Why was I here? Would I be better dead? Why did I exist? What was my purpose if nobody wanted me? Why was I here? Why was I here? Why the fuck was I here? Having a wife and children with a house in the suburbs no longer made any sense—if the truth of human emotion didn't matter, then why did humans themselves? Everything seemed totally, ludicrously meaningless. What was the point of anything? The foundation for my asking these questions was obvious... but I couldn't yet admit that. Powerless to change anything, nihilism was the only way to balm the pain. Instead, I sought answers so that I might validate myself through some philosophical justification. Without it, how could I hold my head up against an entirely antagonistic community that seemed to think having babies was the be-all and end-all of being a good person? Was God's plan that we just keep breeding people until we human-pyramid our way into space like some intergalactic cheer squad? It's far more logical that we just kill anyone below a 4 on the Kinsey Scale and create a master race of human beings who only propagate the species because they're more likely to have considered the philosophical objective of the whole business, not just because they like the sensation of penis in vagina and are blindly led by their basest desires. These thoughts were obvious, and I wanted to talk about them—I was quite sure that any sixteen-year-old leader worth their salt should have known all of that.

Rebecca stopped me just as soon as I could start talking.

"You just can't think about those things," she dismissed.

I was immensely frustrated to find that, even here, amongst the best and brightest, power continued to be handed to those people that willfully ignored what it meant to be human. I had thought, when I was a small child, that after all these thousands of years of civilization we must be living in a golden age. How disappointed I was to discover that not only were we electing those that did not *understand* philosophy, but those that did not even think it *worthwhile*. I had no doubt that I understood greater than any of my peers the mechanics and workings of the world, and yet they couldn't see past my high-pitched voice and socially neglected persona to what lay beneath. How on earth were they supposed to lead humanity if they could not look forward, to question the deepest and darkest parts of what it meant to be alive? How were they leaders at all? I posit once again that our elected leaders are nothing more than figureheads of the status quo, empty vessels, sustained egos. Style over substance. And I, substance with no style. Neglect will do that to you.

On various occasions I can recall being able to hold together a stylish ego for a short amount of time. Usually I could, actually, do this very well, to the point where suddenly I would be overwhelmed with social attention and I would get too excited and lose track of myself and the whole thing would fall apart. I remember one girl looking at me disappointed about an hour after meeting me (I must have been overstimulated and was waving my limp wrists around or something) and her saying, "oh… I thought you were cool…" The breaks in how people treated me were so obvious but trying to develop and maintain that cool ego now required so much mental stamina that I couldn't focus on anything else while doing it, and I refused to become what I despised: one of those beings of pure style over substance.

But that was a long time ago. Today I am very cool just naturally without even trying. And, if anyone were to ask me, off the top of my head I might argue something along the lines that humanity in general is suffering from an existential avoidance crisis, which is to say that I fundamentally disagree with Rebecca and you actually can just think about "those things", and in fact that the issues caused by not thinking about "those things" are a little more urgent to address than my hair or anything going on in a Manual Arts classroom or crocodiles in Far North Queensland. But, nobody does ever ask me anything, so I guess just never mind—let's keep being awful to each other, because certainly the last thing being the centerpiece of conflict did was teach me how to mediate or resolve any of it (I understand only a big man with muscles and weapons and power, whose goal is definitely not to continue the conflict for his own gain, is capable of that) and on with the story.

∴

The end of school was drawing closer and closer, and I was still without any idea of who I was, who I wanted to be.

"How is being a prostitute different from any other job?" I asked Dad one day. "You still sell your body and time for someone else's benefit."

"It's not the same!" he asserted, angrily. "It's about dignity."

I wondered when I would be allowed dignity in these systems. A private humiliation seemed better than a public one. I had taken up my first casual job at Domino's Pizza, performing my job tirelessly, perfectly, those boring hours spent running between sinks washing dirty pans just as fast as I could and the front counter serving customers, some of them horribly rude but even to whom I maintained a polite demeanour, consistently getting 100% on mystery shoppers and even the occasional customer calling back to thank me for my service, all for a few coins that sat in my bank account, not sure what to spend any of it on, but trying to figure out how I could contribute in a meaningful way… but like all my previous successes, my expertise in customer service just seemed to incense my managers and my colleagues. I could not win and my contemporaries would only be happy if I proved their prejudices right, which meant being the stupid, useless poof they all wanted me to be. When I quit after a year of hard work to focus on my final exams, I asked my manager, Sam, for a reference.

"Oh, you think you deserve that, do you?"

I vowed never to work that hard for anyone ever again.

I was angry. I was mad at the whole world, thinking they knew how to educate me when all they had done was hurt me with their ignorance. At the same time, I kept thinking I was missing that vital piece of information, something stopping me from piecing it all together, that unknown thing that kept knocking me down from my blind spot. What was wrong with me that, even when I got everything right, I still failed?

What did I have to do to prove myself as worthy and capable? I began to believe, quite simply, what everyone seemed to want me to believe: that I wasn't.

One day the Premier, Anna Bligh, came to the Academy. I knew nothing about her and I hated her. I wanted to slash her throat. I understood why two thousand years earlier, a man who had spent his entire life working in a coalmine tried to slash the throat of Hadrian. In his wisdom, Hadrian took that man on as his personal serviceman. Would my frustrations ever be understood as such? Did I need to pull out a knife to be heard or acknowledged?

Occasionally we had to sit exams that didn't go towards our graduating scores, but exams where the results were combined to surmise the performance averages of schools so rich parents could decide where to send their little brats and deepen the class divide. Well, I knew already I could answer every single question on the sheet in front of me. What benefit did my hard work bring to me? Nothing. Again, I sat back in my chair and folded my arms. I sat like that for two hours, refusing to answer a single question. The system was broken and fucked up and I would not participate any further in activities that only served to help other people. Too much had been taken from me. I would not be measured on their arbitrary criteria of intelligence and success, which apparently counted for nothing if I wasn't masculine, the one thing that everyone wanted from me but that nobody could be bothered to teach me. My truth and sensitivity denied, I would not be a slave to people that simply did not understand. My non-compliance in participating in these exams caused a great confusion. I did my best to explain this to my parents, to my teachers, to Principal Jose, but how could they understand my revolt? I could not yet say the specific words I needed to say. My kind had been silenced for so long.

I'm gay, and you don't respect me.

∴

I don't remember much of our school formal, the boys and girls pairing off, another rite of passage in which my truth had no inclusion.

I do remember playing spin-the-bottle at the after party, the bottle pointing at me and another boy named

Roo.

I remember someone else saying: "Two guys can't kiss. If two girls kiss, it's bi, but if two guys kiss, it's gay." He was from the Redlands, a boy who had come with the daughter of Karen Williams, the Mayor of the Redlands, as if my homeland was haunting me at every turn.

I remember wondering whose side Karen would be on.

I remember how nobody said anything.

And I remember how Roo, big, burly and ever-masculine, in front of everyone, leant over, looked me in the eyes, and gave me a short, sweet peck on the lips.

[Enter CHORUS].

CHORUS: May it be my aim to be reverent and
holy by day and on through
the night, and, rejecting all
customs that transgress justice,
to know the gods!
Let Justice come for all to see, let her
come sword in hand,
stabbing through the throat to
his death the godless,
the lawless, the unjust man.

[Enter DIONYSUS, dragging in chains ANNA BLIGH, KAREN WILLIAMS, and the corpse of JOH BJELKE PETERSEN.]

DIONYSUS: Yes, yes, we've heard all that before.
Well! What do you have to say for
yourselves?
Tormenting those without power, using
them for your own gain?

JOH: A.

DIONYSUS: Pathetic. Too far, you say!
Only now that it's your life, or rather
legacy, on the line.
And you? You say you lead the march
towards progress?
What did you care for the voices of the
downtrodden?

ANNA: A.

DIONYSUS: Oh, well that's quite good actually.
                 Ok, you can go.

[ANNA BLIGH is unchained and exits.]

DIONYSUS: And you. At least you don't lie about
                       your allegiances.
                 What have you to say for yourself?
                 For your betrayals against your fellow
                       man?
                 Even those helpless children?

KAREN: A.

DIONYSUS: Sorry, I wasn't listening.
                 I guess your issues just don't affect me.
                 Aren't really relevant, you know.
                 You should work on that.
                 Followers, upon them!

[JOANNE ROWLING and the BACCHANTS launch upon JOH BJELKE PETERSEN and KAREN WILLIAMS, ripping off their heads and devouring them.]

DIONYSUS: Blood and gore! How's that for the real
                       world?
                 What a mess you've made me make.

[DIONYSUS and the CHORUS exit, leaving a pool of viscera.]

III

And This Muscle Piggy Puffed Some Meth

"I'm gay."

The words toppled clumsily out of my mouth.

For months I had sweat in silence. Moments came and went, gaps in conversation when I thought, *say it, now, just spit it out, get it over with,* my adrenaline through the roof as I sat stuck in my own head, but I could never build up the courage. This truth should have emerged all those years ago—*you can't play with the boys, you have to play with the girls*—it had been so obvious what they were pointing to—what I had been pointing to. Why had no one helped me? Why the taboo?

I had become paralysed, buried alive by the last fifteen years, so that there felt like no good or natural time to bring the revelation to light, no casual way to make the admission. For fifteen years I had lived in this trap.

I had to escape.

One night, I managed it.

Only an hour earlier my shirt had been drenched with sweat as I poked nervously at my food, the family around the dinner table, urging myself to do the one thing I knew I had to do but somehow couldn't. The silence had been inflicted on me so long that it had become both a prison and a sanctuary. Speaking up would destroy both. Did I really want to leave comfort in exchange for the truth? I would be entering an unknown reality, and once I had torn down the illusion, there was no putting it back up. Not that there ever seemed enough time to build myself up to action and cross that threshold. Before I knew it everyone had eaten, dinner was over, and I still hadn't mustered the courage. I went to my room and lay in bed, upset. I couldn't bear another night in silence. I listened as my parents washed up, showered, and finally called out goodnight.

I had to do it.

"Wait!" I cried. I leaped out of bed, ran through the house, stopping in their doorway, "I have to tell you something."

"What is it?"

Mum and Dad sat in bed, staring at me. My heart was racing. My underarms were drenched. Could I really do it?

Just say it. Say it!

That moment of silence felt like an age as I hoisted the colossal weight of those words from the depths of my being.

My tongue felt as solid as concrete. I couldn't pronounce the syllables at all. I had practiced when I was home alone, *I'm gay, I'm gay, I'm gay,* but even then, the words had seemed unnatural, like they somehow avoided the meaning and confidence I wanted to put into them. Now, with witnesses, it was close to impossible. They refused to roll off the tongue. Like complex words in a foreign language, my mouth didn't seem to know how to unleash them.

"I'm—ga—y."

And yet, those strange little noises escaped my mouth, close enough together to carry what I wanted to say.

I had finally done it.

"I knew it!" Mum shouted.

And Dad, after a pause: "why?"

"There's not really a reason. I just am."

"But why?" he persisted, not angry, just confused.

"It's not a choice, Dad. I hoped for a long time I would be straight, but... that's just not how it works."

He nodded.

"Ok. Just don't change. Don't become one of those..."

"What?"

"Sissies."

"I'm just going to be me, Dad."

If only it were that easy.

They told me they loved me, and I went to bed exhilarated.

I didn't see Dad for a few days. He obviously had a lot to process and spent all his time working in the shed. The buzzing of power tools might as well have been the engines of his brain working overtime, processing what I'm sure was a difficult chore: that his only son would *not* be finding a girlfriend, getting married, having his grandkids.

I kept replaying Mum's words in my mind.

I knew it.

I thought by telling them I was gay I had shattered their illusions about what was real, not given them information they had already known but decided to ignore, the very same information that had been hidden from me and deprived me of both a healthy childhood and adolescence. I thought back to how Dad had silenced me at the dinner table a decade earlier, upset that I had called Amy a poof. I wondered to what extent Mum had followed his denial of the existence of homosexuality, turning a blind eye, choosing instead to be a good wife, to submit to his reality. I felt anger that I should be doing such basic work towards illuminating the reality of sexuality for both my family and society.

Despair over our own existences certainly makes us bury obvious truths. Masochistic for meaning, we give ourselves over to existing powers so easily. My mother had given herself over to my father, and my father to an oppressive society. If they had known my sexuality intuitively, I supposed they had not thought it worth fighting off so much oppression on a hunch. That job fell to me. And now, all I wanted to do was chase my desires, those that had been repressed so long they now came out overflowing. Après moi, le déluge. But I was seventeen years old and I had no idea how to get what I wanted, had no clear idea of what that even was.

Well, a lot of things can change in a decade. I was no longer the confused boy at the dinner table, unsure what *poof* meant or how it applied to me, wondering why everyone was angry. Another ten years and where would I be?

∴

I walk into the pig's rented apartment and claim it as my own. He has come up to visit on a work trip and he won't be getting much sleep as I make him puff, frying his piggy brains.

A man somewhere loves him.
I do not.
I could.
I feel the bud of those feelings and suppress them, give them no oxygen.

He is beautiful but he shall have nothing but my cruelty.

He disrobes at my command. I chain his balls to one corner of the bed and with a collar chain his neck to the other, ass up. His arms and legs are free to flail helplessly, but he cannot move and cannot get away. I fuck him, feeling his stretched-out pussy loose around my cock, then shove my fist up there deep until he is moaning and begging me to stop.

I drag him to the balcony, tie him to a chair, and turn on the light so all the apartments in the opposing building can see what a faggot he is, gagging and drooling on himself.

I stare at him from a dark corner, watching the panic in his eyes.

After a good half-hour of this exposure I loose him from the chair, tie a rope around his erection, lead him to the boot of his own car, order him in, take his wallet and drive us to the ATM. I open the boot to ask his pin and then get out a few hundred dollars in cash. I take photos of all his cards and driver's license.

Afterwards he cooks me dinner in chains. I let him drool looking at my cock while I eat but I don't let him touch me.

I go to sleep but he is so wired he can't and instead stays up watching porn.

∴

I had to escape Brisbane. I had to escape Australia.

My country hated me, and despite my best efforts at memory loss I was consumed with rage toward it.

I would save for a year and leave for London.

I was envious of men like Salman Rushdie. What a great blessing a fatwa on my head might be, as if my enemies would ever name their hate publicly and provide me that helping hand. But as my oppression was so well hidden, I had no opportunity to react, to change the narrative against me. They were clever enough to only attack me in secret so that I appeared to be the one that was dramatic and unhinged.

There had to be someplace better.

I worked only that I might flee.

But first I had to get a job, and that involved the most terrifying prospect: a job interview. Having to convince *other people* that *I was capable*.

This was (almost entirely) impossible, and I couldn't stomach any further rejection.

Were my intelligence and sensitivity not consistently considered to be weaknesses?

I had excelled in my studies and it meant nothing.

I had performed my previous customer service job to an exceptional standard and all I received in exchange was hatred.

I had managed to pinpoint the philosophical concepts underneath my sexuality and the oppressive political forces against it, I had even weaponised existentialism against the anxiety that paralysed me, breaking down the very mental illness that inflicted me and that nobody else could understand or advise me on, and all this I did as a child with no training in psychology.

I was a detail-oriented results-driven self-motivated go-getting team-player.

Yet clearly, I was missing something.

Something was wrong with me.

What was I supposed to say to someone interviewing me?

"I have an extreme anxiety disorder due to having been ostracised since birth on the basis of prejudice to the extent that all my successes just cause me further hate, distress, and abjection. I am extremely competent and continuously make meaningful contributions but it is the fault of a flawed society that I am unable to find any traction."

I was so heavily gaslit that I couldn't say any of that with a modicum of confidence. Even with confidence, it sounded delusional, particularly to a hiring manager that just wants an employee with minimal neuroses. And even if they knew I was right, it only categorised me as trouble. Why would anyone want to get into some weird conflict on behalf of some fucked up, anxious teenager?

But I didn't know how to lie, either—to say, "oh yes, I am much beloved in my community, very popular at school, widely appreciated for all I have to offer."

That was anything but the truth.

And then, even if I could successfully lie, I knew it would only give birth to a burgeoning paranoia—how long until they found out I was a loser, a worthless faggot that had never deserved to be included? People want to know where you've come from, your story, how you fit into the world—there was, quite simply, no easy way to explain my history.

A job interview became my most hated, dreaded thing in the entire world.

I filled with rage at the very prospect of someone else judging me when it felt like there were no right answers, and it became the crux upon which any semblance of ego I might have been able to pull together completely collapsed. Simple questions like, "on a scale of zero to ten, how good are your customer service skills?" became impossible to answer. Judging from my time at Domino's, I thought a ten, but considering the customers that would harass me for my sexuality (impossible to serve without upsetting) and the fact that my previous managers refused to give me a reference meant I couldn't stand by this. I was also wildly aware of how narcissistic it would be to actually say ten, and so, knowing I had to lie but having absolutely no idea what they wanted to hear from me, I said "five." *Five*. Existence crumbled around me. I was sweating and my face was red and I couldn't think, my brain felt heavy like lead, adrenaline pumping through my veins.

"Sorry, but you're not what we're looking for," I heard, again and again, unable to explain the incommunicable truth and unable to lie.

I don't know how but I scraped in a job at a supermarket around the corner from home, scanning item after item at the checkout for forty hours a week. I could feel my mind atrophying and the only exception to that was when it was morally disheartening.

It would always start with a customer noticing that the special prices weren't scanning correctly. I already knew the special prices didn't scan correctly because the store manager, Wayne, did it on purpose to make more money. I had made my thoughts crystal clear to Wayne on this.

"One day you'll understand how the real world works. We need to make money somehow."

Not wanting to lose the one job I had, I remained silent, subjecting myself to angry customers instead.

The real stinger here was that I was not considered worthy of the privilege of adjusting prices on the computer because, and I must point out the heavy irony, *I might steal*. The result was that I had to stand around getting lectured and abused about ethical trading by customers the store was stealing from, a lecture I agreed with but had no power to implement, waiting five or ten minutes for Wayne or another manager to finally show up and change the prices because, as I've said, apparently I as a lowly checkout person was by default the morally dubious one. Did no good men exist? I was trapped in a world of monsters that despite their preaching of goodness had no understanding of it, and so it was reinforced to me, time and time again, that our society was built on nothing more than betrayal and backstabbing, and that I was the incorrect and naïve one for actually attempting to practice my do-gooder ethics. I would cry on my way home from work at the knowledge that if I were to ever make it on my own I would need to take similar advantage of people. But I didn't have the heart yet for such hypocrisy, to wear a smile on my face while hiding a dagger in my sleeve.

The thought that I might find a boyfriend was the one thing that pushed me through. Socially incompetent but learning how to fit again into my own body, I stood at that checkout and tried to smile, tried to believe I was meant for something more than a henchman in someone else's scam, in which it seemed particularly unfair that I would be forced to be complicit and not even reap the profits. An awkward boy about my age started coming through the checkout. His cheeks were pockmarked, a sign that his own adolescence hadn't been so kind, but my breath quickened when I served him, my face flushed red, both of us unsure what to say, a nervous tension between us.

One day he gave me his number.

I texted him after work and met him in the park.

"Can I hug you?" he asked.

I let him, turning my head, scared people were watching from their houses.

"Let's go for a walk up through the bush," I said.

I broke into a sweat as we crossed the busy main road together. *There go the fags,* I could hear the drivers hurling abuse in their minds.

But as soon as we were up there, out of sight, a patch of grass behind some concrete water tanks, I leapt on him, my tongue in his mouth, my hands feeling an impossible bulge underneath his jeans. It was the first time I had ever really touched someone, kissed someone. I was rock hard but I didn't let him suck me, didn't suck him, too scared of catching something, and too much of a romantic. I didn't want to be the boy that lost his virginity in the bush, especially with an even more awkward mess of a human being than I was. That didn't stop me kissing him for hours. I needed it. I needed to feel wanted.

Afterwards I texted him that I couldn't do it again, and he got upset and blocked me—probably rightly. He never came through my checkout again, except for one instance with his mother where he was obviously unable to tell her that I must be avoided. I could tell he was in great pain, which gave me no pleasure.

I worked at the supermarket for about a year and saved a little over five thousand dollars. Not much, but enough to escape. I bought my plane ticket to London.

∴

The next time my pig comes to visit I tie him to the bed, put a hood on him, and invite a stranger on Grindr to use him. I leave them together in the room, unsupervised, my pig totally helpless. After a while the stranger emerges.

"Do you ever bottom?" he asks me.

"Sometimes," I laugh. The stranger is jerking his cock, staring at me. He does not want to cum in the pig. He wants to cum in me.

"Not tonight," I say.

The stranger goes back into the room to finish himself off. The cruel thing would have been to take the load for myself, to hold myself above my pig as the object of true desire, but the knowledge of that reality is enough for me. I do not need to enact it.

But once the stranger leaves and I untie my pig from his predicament, I make sure to let him know: he wanted to cum in me. The gift of semen deep inside him becomes tainted, no longer a pure exchange, but one that will impregnate him with desire for me.

I'm hot, baby.

∴

In the month leading up to my flight I finally turned eighteen. I was terrified as I drank a bottle of wine, trying not to throw up on the bus into town. I had to be as intoxicated as possible, not just to overcome my anxiety, but because I couldn't afford drinks at a bar. I couldn't help but do the math: a single drink was worth the same as an hour of my time standing at a checkout. My time was worth more than either of those things. I just didn't know how to prove that to anyone.

Terrified, drunk, on my own on the dancefloor at the Beat, I made eye contact with a handsome man—muscular and dark, only a year or two older than myself. He bought me a drink and we moved into a secluded dark corner where we started kissing.

Then a man tapped me on the shoulder.

"Hey, you guys need to stop kissing. You're making my friends uncomfortable."

"Uhh… what?" I asked.

"We're not homophobic," he said. "We're here to support our friend. She's just come out as a lesbian."

He pointed to the one girl amongst a group of guys glaring like they wanted to beat the shit out of us.

We shamefully retreated to the smoking area.

I should have stood up to them, I should have called security, but I had never been allowed to take up space and I hadn't learned how to, even in a gay bar—and people see that. They see the weakness, the vulnerability, and they use it to stick the knife in and control you. Besides, *gay panic* was still an acceptable legal defense: the shock of realising a person was gay was a legal excuse to assault them. In that moment, kissing a boy I was attracted to, I was legally liable for the comfort of any weak people nearby and forced to bow to them, as if they were the ones that carried my strength. But I learned from that injury. The problem was, the more prepared I was to stand up for myself the less people attempted to control me, which was nice on one hand, but on the other, left me with deeply buried scars that each required some form of retaliation but no one on which I could fairly exhume them. With every act of abasement against me my rage grew.

In the smoking area, I kept kissing this man. He told me his name was Dom, and we dated ever so briefly, a few nights spent in each other's embrace. He was upset when I told him I was leaving, but by coincidence, he would be visiting London about a month after I arrived.

∴

The pig is closing himself off to me. I have been too cruel to him, pushed him to the edge. I sense it in the way he writes, direct and final, with full stops at the end of each message. His agitation seeps through but I refuse to be responsible for anyone else's emotions. I will make him love me and the pain will be all his. The truth comes out the day before he leaves on holiday with his boyfriend: he will be getting a new number while overseas and will not be contactable. I wonder if he means to cut himself off from me completely. I do not know what to say. I do not give him access to my feelings. The third Michael toyed with my feelings too far and my pig, the fourth Michael, is a necessary reaction. My experiment. I have become a man of my people: silent. On sex and my relationships, what is there to tell those that fall for me? *You'll figure it out.* But no man can exist against my reactionary silence: the pig crumbles, tells me how without me a void is left that was not there before, how on our first real night together when he was wired and stayed up masturbating he wished he had fallen asleep holding me, in my arms, his only regret, and I know it is only through cruelty and denial that in him I have created desire. I feel that worm of conscience in my belly. I have in some small way accomplished retribution. The pig loves his partner of a decade but desires me, though in an absolute switching of the roles to the Michael before him, the pain belongs to him and I will carry none of it. I want to see how far the pig will go for me, if he will burden himself with the same pain as I did, our ritual of suffering, if only so I can finally say to his broken soul: welcome to the club, *welcome to the real world.*

∴

I landed in London as if I had lived there my whole life. I leapt from station to station, carriage to carriage, the complex crossroads of tube tunnels nothing compared to the abyssal map of the unknown I had so long been creating. Standing on the left of the moving stairways, I shared in the contempt for anyone who blocked the right, wondering if they had just arrived here and, if not, how much longer they would survive. The afternoon sun was warm as I pulled my bright red suitcase along. The world felt new, and everything was glowing, myself especially.

At the hostel I was assigned a bunk in a crammed room of about fifteen beds at the cost of about ten pounds a night. I made some new friends, all Australians, who invited me out drinking, but I was too exhausted. The only one I remember well was a blonde girl called (I think) Leish. I asked what food was around and she took me downstairs to a convenience store where I bought a refrigerated packaged sandwich for dinner. Everyone went out, and, on my first night in London, I went to sleep.

I rose the next day at 6am as if my entire body clock had been reset. More importantly, I was happy to be alive, my usual anxiety quelled by this new beginning. For the longest time, life had somehow become nothing more than a daily chore or punishment, as if I had been required to exist without passion, as if surviving in such a state of despair and torment had been a virtue rather than a terrible waste of my own innate vivacity. I journeyed into town with absolutely no plan in mind except exploring my new home. I got off at Piccadilly Circus because it sounded familiar—I had done no research before coming to this city, trusting whatever call had unconsciously reached me—and wandered aimlessly, eventually arriving at Trafalgar Square. The town seemed to coerce my path, leading me to all the right places. I was reading on a bench behind St. Martin-in-the-Fields church when an older man in his fifties or sixties started a conversation with me. He noticed my accent and I told him I had just arrived, that, yes, I was all alone, and that I couldn't believe how beautiful the city was, to which he invited me to come out to Oxford with him some time to see the architecture. I told him that sounded lovely. He gave me his number, which I kept, though I would never call, and he wandered off to see what other young men had strayed into his den. It was the first time I felt power as a lonely youth, something in my wide-eyed appraisal of this new terrain that suggested I was vulnerable, but it became obvious that my vulnerability was attractive to some men and they had something to offer me in exchange for it. Inspired by this potential as I was, I could not figure out how to take myself up on the transaction, for despite my long-held view that any and all relationships are transactionary, I could not yet allow myself to be so mercenary. Thus it was my very insistence on naivety, the same thing that attracted these men to me, that for the moment prevented me from participating with them. But something in my spirit was stirred behind the church that day. I was no abject terror in this land. This man approaching me was proof of that. Here I was beautiful.

∴

I torture the pig until he is almost crying. I want to send him over that edge. I want him to know how I've felt.

"You can cry," I yell, holding back tears of my own.

I whip him with a burnt rope that Michael had used on me and he gets angry, roaring, but the chains give nothing. He gives nothing. It is too much for me to push him any further.

Later, on his knees, not from physical pain but emotional, a few tears roll down his face.

"Why would anyone treat you like that? I don't understand."

∴

I wanted to get out of the hostel as soon as possible. Sharing a room with so many other bunks made me feel exposed. To be fair, I was not used to people treating me kindly. I quickly found a room to rent at Leytonstone, with a bed and a wardrobe and a great window overlooking a sunny, leafy courtyard. The night before I was to move in, Leish and some others took me across the city to Brick Lane with its hundreds of Indian restaurants. We walked up and down, drunk, haggling with the waiters out the front on what deal they would do us. Eventually we made a deal: a free entrée and three free rounds of drinks. The ground level was full so he took us down to the basement. Only one other table occupied the space and after a few minutes seated next to them we realised they were fellow Australians. Not only that, they were living in Leytonstone. I'm not sure how it happened but by some unlikely and pointless miracle, about twelve hours before I would have met them anyway, this is how I met my new housemates, seated next to me in the basement of one of hundreds of Indian restaurants, of all the places in London to have dinner.

The next day I was not sure if it had been a dream. I pulled my suitcase across town and, entering the house, there they were again, those bright and familiar faces from the evening before: three Australian girls and a South African man. The arbitrary meeting the night before seemed to be London laying down my red carpet. Not a red carpet of celebration, necessarily, but one of personal growth. I took it as all storytellers who enjoy synchronicity would: as an indication that I was on the right path.

My housemates were kind and fun, but early on, I remember a run-in with one of the girls.

"That's gay," she had said—a derogatory put-down of, I can't remember what.

I remembered how before I knew anything about my sexuality, language had already taught me that being gay was a bad thing. I had hated myself before I even understood myself.

"You shouldn't use *gay* like that," I said, my voice shaking, "it's—"

She turned to me with fury in her eyes.

"Do you really want to try this?" she screamed at me in front of the other housemates.

My face turned red and I went silent.

But I never heard her use *gay* like that again. I

might not have won that battle in the moment, but I was proud of myself for trying. It had taken me so many years to learn to speak up. To take up space. For my nature to not be a casual insult.

Generally, we all got along quite well. On one occasion I got so drunk I blocked the sink with my vomit. I openly admitted my fault and cleaned it up upon awakening the next morning. On another occasion, the South African got so drunk he covered the bathroom walls with vomit. He profusely denied it the next day, but when he thought no one was around, I heard him sneak into the bathroom and clean it up.

I had to start work as quickly as possible to avoid cutting into my hard-earned savings. The hostel I had stayed at offered a service for fill-in hotel event staff, a service provided entirely by underpaid internationals, and I attended the two-day unpaid training course with Leish. At the end of these two days, we sat a multiple-choice exam while our supervisors smoked cigarettes outside. The class spoke candidly with each other, sharing answers, and as I glanced at Leish's paper, I noticed she had almost every answer wrong. I gestured to her answer sheet, then to mine.

"Copy mine," I said.

"Just let me put what I think it is," she said, with apparently not a doubt in her head about what she was capable of.

I nodded. I might have had the right answers, but she had the confidence, and I knew enough already that intelligence didn't really count for anything. I passed the exam and was hired for baseline duties. Leish, full of confidence but with almost every answer wrong, was hired as a manager. I had thought it was Leish that had to copy me, but really, I needed to start copying her. But I didn't want to trade truth and knowledge for confidence. I wanted to learn to do both.

In my first deployment, a wedding, alone in a sea of visa holders, I was overcome by panic. How many of us were there? One hundred? Two hundred? Leish was nowhere to be seen, probably off managing another event, so I was totally alone. We were ushered through winding windowless hallways and dressed in unfamiliar uniforms. Then we waited, I'm not sure how long, in those underground corridors. Maybe an hour, maybe two. I felt a nervous tension, like a soldier before battle attempting to remain stoic. The wedding party arrived. We were flung into action. People were carried off in every direction, siphoned into various placements, the managers more flustered than I was, torrenting abuse to keep us in order. As per usual, getting yelled at made me feel like I was in trouble, fuelled my anxiety further, and my brain shut down completely, the adrenaline shooting through my veins, heart racing, body working overtime.

I was selected to hold a tray of cocktails. A simple enough duty but probably something that required practice—I'd never balanced a tray before, and we had done no practical training. I stared at the drinks and passing guests in horror, hundreds of them moving from one end of the hotel to the other in a slow procession that took the better part of an hour, doing my best to keep the tray stable every time a drink was removed. I was already physically exhausted from the many hours of anxiety through which my body had been attacking itself—and I watched terrified, helpless, as my weak wrist failed me on yet another front, going numb, the tray tilting, the drinks falling in slow motion, my face going red, humiliated before the glasses could even smash on the floor, the guests gasping. One of the managers dragged me out the back in contempt.

"Just stay here and wash glasses."

Here I spent the rest of the night, hours upon hours, polishing the same glassware, the managers screaming at me for more, more, more; the guests not having enough drinks, and the anger with which they directed this shortcoming toward me made it seem as if the whole situation was my fault despite my never having set foot in this hotel before. I was totally drained, exhausted, beaten down, all for what? Five pounds an hour? The boy next to me was in an equal amount of despair but had already found his coping mechanism. He considerately offered me a sip of his flask, which helped my nerves but not my tiredness. The only escape from this mundane torment was that every now and then I would rejoin the coffle to carry a plate, one slave for each of the guests to make sure everyone was served dinner at the exact same moment (a magical experience from their perspective), and then back to the glasses where my abusers would oscillate between screaming at me that I could not polish fast enough or that I was polishing too fast and leaving blemishes. After twelve or so hours I couldn't take it anymore. To get screamed at over something as trivial as glassware made me want to die. I desperately wanted to be as confident as Leish but I certainly did not think I could build my confidence subject to such conditions. I also did the math: I'd earned maybe fifty quid, not even half my rent for the week. I didn't think I could do this three times a week just for shelter, then again for food, then again so that, at the end of it, I might afford some small enjoyment. The trap was obvious. My minimum wage was just enough to keep me alive but not enough to afford me any opportunity for growth or escape. For most people, their lives might have been motivation enough to do this, to make money just to keep on living, but I hated my life. Escaping to London had improved things, given me a sense of freedom, but I still had no interest in continuing living just to prolong the current setup of being abused; the combination of suffering and boredom was not worth the privilege. Besides, this employment was not building my confidence, it was making me want to throw myself off a bridge. It was not that I did not want to put in hard work. I believe I'd made it clear that I'd work harder than anyone given an actual incentive, but it was like I was supposed to enjoy working hard for no appreciation and no reward. I came to realise that my laziness was not an innate flaw within me but again a symptom of my abjection. In those hours of remedial work this became as crystal clear as the glasses I was polishing. I was done proving myself. Anyone that wanted my hard work would have to pay upfront, and so, sometime after midnight, when the managers were distracted, I crept away through the back corridors, found my bag, got changed, and threw my uniform into a corner. I emerged into the wedding where the merrymakers were still carrying on, the other slaves still bending over for someone else's pleasure, either blind to their prison or not believing themselves capable of escape, and passing a table covered in large boxes of macarons by the exit – a gift for the guests to take with them – I stole an entire box. All staff, all slaves, were supposed to leave via the back exit. I walked right out the front lobby. Tears streamed down my face as I wandered through the dark, foreign streets of London, caught the two buses on the long journey out to Leytonstone, eating my macarons, a thief in the night. Better a thief than a slave, I thought.

I came back to my room as the sun was rising, and pulling the curtains closed, I passed into a cold fever that lasted weeks. Every few days I attempted the walk to the grocery store, stopping to rest on benches as I went, finally returning so exhausted that I thought I was certainly going to die. The South African would occasionally check on me, bringing honey-lemon tea. (Today whenever I am sick I will boil the kettle, slice up some lemon, pour some honey in a mug and think of him.) I slept for a whole fortnight, and just as I was starting to feel better, Dom, the man I had met in Brisbane, arrived in London on a holiday.

He visited me one afternoon in my room, bringing groceries and flowers to make me feel better. I could tell he loved me, so in a cold sweat, I lost my virginity to him. I was on all fours on the bed and, him standing behind me, I told him to put it in. It was painful and I cried. I didn't know how to relax. No one had taught me anything. All I knew was that it was the right time, but still, nothing felt easy. I jerked off afterwards, him holding me, but I don't remember feeling any real pleasure or excitement: just fear. I asked if he wanted to be my boyfriend and he said no, it would be too hard on opposite sides of the world. Move to London, I said, but he couldn't, or wouldn't. I managed to walk him to the station as the sun was setting and kissed him goodbye. I watched as the train carried him away, down into the dark tunnels. Still dizzy from the illness and feeling as though I might faint, I sat down on a bench, bracing my nerves for the walk back home, the late summer sun low in the sky, the warmth grazing the back of my neck. Winter was setting in.

In those days I enjoyed the dark and the rain and the cold, a reflection of my permanent internal condition (the brutal summers and oppressive sun of my homeland could have been enough to drive me into a murderous craze like that of Meursault), but I was not prepared for the descent into even bleaker poverty. I suddenly required a root canal that cut into most of my savings so that, sitting in a dentist chair late at night, alone in a building with a strange man in some strange part of London, my mouth wide open as he took what little I had and I stared out the great window at the yellow full moon hung there amidst the darkened silhouette of chimneys and terrace spikes, London became a horror, the very mould encroaching so rapidly so that one morning I found it had covered, seemingly overnight, both my bathroom bag and my shoes. In the daytime I wandered the streets of Soho and, slim and malnourished as I was, I purchased my first jockstrap in the smallest size I could find and still it did not fit. In the evenings I frequented the gay bars, met one boy my age, a student named Ben who became my first boyfriend, travelled with him down to cold Bournemouth, made love on the beach, even stayed with him briefly when I ran out of money, but London had its fill of me, and I of it.

∴

I tie the pig to his couch, gagged and exposed, and finish most of the bottle of champagne from his fridge. One glass I leave on the kitchen counter for his boyfriend to find. He might need it when he sees the love of his life like this.

I can just make out his muffled words: "you know if you do this it's over, right?"

"Bye piggy," I laugh, and walk out the front door.

His boyfriend is due any minute. I half expect to pass him in the corridor on my way out.

In the Uber back to Josh's I think about how, if we get through this, I might give him his first kiss the next time I see him. I think about messaging him that. I type it, and then delete it without sending. Then a message from the pig comes through. It's a photo. He's out of bondage. The kitchen counter is clean.

"I knew you'd get out. How?"

"Strength."

Then there's a feud. He's angry at me. He can't understand why I'd do something like that.

"Do you want me out of your life?"

"Of course not," I say.

We don't speak for a week. I refuse to chase him. Refuse to care. He's my meth pig and he'll destroy himself for me. That is all he is good for.

Finally, he reappears. He wants answers.

Do I keep hurting him? Turn the knife? Perpetuate his suffering?

That was my plan all along.

To show him that the only person he can rely on is himself. That everyone else will abandon him.

"Just remember, every action has a reaction," Josh says, using some of my own favourite words against me.

I decide I cannot punish him anymore.

I explain everything I've been through.

I explain that I wanted to use the same power and sadism that had been used on me. An experiment, so to speak.

I explain how at the nadir of my suffering I found

myself, found the courage and power to remake myself, and that this is the gift I want to give him.

I explain that maybe ultimately I have failed him, because it was with a deep hatred of the man who hurt me that I was able to do this: how can he hate me when I have revealed my true heart?

I also explain the people I've lost to crystal meth—how I warned them—how they did not heed me.

"I told you I was happy to hold your hand on that path towards self-destruction," I say to the pig, "if that's where you really wanted to go. Nothing else has ever worked. But I've learned that you need to let people make their mistakes. I didn't know how else to help you, except to show you where this path led."

In the moment he is mad. He feels betrayed by me. He is not sure he agrees with my strategy. I am not sure I agree with my strategy. But I'm also not sure I care anymore. It's just something to do.

But he comes around.

"The more I think about it, the more appreciative I am of you shining a light on the things I need to change," says the pig, "Sometimes a good kick in the arse from someone who knows exactly where to kick is all it takes."

"One thing my daddy told me, the really bad one, was that I'd learn to love the pain," I say, "more than anything, I hate that he was right, without ever understanding what he was doing. Or did he? I don't know. Sometimes I feel like a puppet. I hate him so much. In that pain, I found so much growth. More growth than I've ever experienced. I wanted to give you that same feeling of growth but I didn't want to lock you into the anger I feel."

"I don't get the feeling that he was trying to make

you a better person. It was for his own enjoyment and he was trying to coax you into believing his mantra. I think you came at this from a different angle and whilst you still got benefit from my downfall, ultimately you wanted to show me what a downfall could really look like… I'm not sure your daddy had your experience or was trying to impart any wisdom on you."

"I think you're right about all of that."

"Well if that's the case, he is pure evil, and he deserves everything that is coming his way. And you are one of the strongest people in this world to have been able to stand up to him, through all of that pain and suffering but also addictive enjoyment, and say, *no more, fuck you, now it's your time to burn.*"

"Thank you for doing for me what he never could."

"And what's that?"

"I don't know how to put it into words exactly."

"Believe in you."

"I guess. When he called me a worthless faggot I think he actually believed it."

"I've been thinking I wished I could watch you whipping me… seeing me squirm and scream and see what your face looked like… if you were hard… if you were smiling and laughing. But now I don't think I would want to see that, because I think I would see a lot of pain and heartache."

"Right again."

"I am completely lost for words. I want to say more than I'm sorry for what he did to you because that doesn't mean anything. But that's horrific. No one deserves that. I just want to lift you up as high as I can. And help you see what a beautiful person you are, without fancy cars or houses or books... Just you."

And all the pain from all I've wrote so far, all I've still to write... just kind of... vanishes. All I had to do was torture the love out of a pig.

∴

I returned home and found myself, for the first time since my childhood, quite thankful for the sun, but also for the first time since my childhood, back in the Redlands.

And this time in debt. I owed my parents two-thousand dollars.

Meanwhile, my sister got engaged to her high school sweetheart. Typical of my family who all married, had children, and walked into their working-class careers straight out of school. She planned to have a small ceremony overseas in Fiji. I explained to my parents, quite simply, that I would not be able to afford to go unless they paid for me. I could see the frustration on their faces, wondering why their child, by all criteria now a man, was incapable of making any real money. They reluctantly agreed to pay for me.

In Fiji, a few things happened.

Firstly, on the night before the wedding, my family were all gathered around, drinking and talking politics.

"You'd have to be a bloody idiot to vote Labor," my Nain (Welsh for *grandma*) laughed.

"I vote Labor," I glared at her, "I'd like to get married one day too."

The room went quiet and the topic changed.

Then, drunk by the beach and approaching midnight, some cows were running along the sand. I gave chase with a few of the groomsmen, Adam and Travis. A hundred meters up we stopped at a campfire where a few of the locals were hanging out.

"Do you know where we can buy some weed?" we asked.

"Yeah, follow us."

They led us along some dark roads to a closed bar. From the shadows a great black man emerged, towering over us. The locals explained what we wanted.

"No problem," said the giant, leaning in close to me and then whispering, "get rid of the girls and I'll sell you some."

I turned to Travis and Adam.

"I'll handle it, just take the girls across the street."

They all left and I was alone with him.

"I like boys," he continued whispering, his hands feeling their way around my backside, both of us hidden by the darkness, "do you like jewelry?"

"Yes."

He pulled a ring off his colossal finger, his lips and his breath against my neck.

"Here."

It was massive, and I held it loosely around my thumb as I paid for the weed.

"Come back and see me. I'll be here."

On the walk back to the hotel, I told Adam and Travis what happened.

"That big guy?"

"Nah, no way."

"Seriously, look at this ring he gave me!"

"Don't lie, man."

"Yeah, that's not cool."

It was impossible to convince them that I might have been desirable, impossible to reveal to them that homosexuality was everywhere, impossible to show them that the most masculine of men were not necessarily interested in the most feminine women, but that it might be a slim, young boy like myself that they want to hold and kiss and penetrate.

I gave up trying to convince them.

Back at the hotel, I put my chain through the ring and wore it around my neck. Then I ordered room service, a milkshake, and the boy who brought it, Naruma, flirted with me.

"I was watching you today on the beach," he said, "you are so beautiful."

And yet, I felt totally invisible. I left the room and spent a few hours with him in the gardens, talking, flirting... did we kiss? I don't remember.

But this trip was not about me. This trip was about my sister finding the love of her life. Except, it was always so easy for her, wasn't it? Everyone always saw her. *Your sister is so cool, your sister is so hot, why aren't you like that?* No one ever saw me. No one even believed that I could be attractive. It's not like I needed everything to be about me. But some things are about me, and I don't know why that's so hard for people to acknowledge or believe, and why those things always had to be taken away from me or denied.

Amy got married. The weather on the beach that morning was perfect. The water was flat and clear, and the waves washed softly up onto the shore. As she walked down the aisle she was glowing. I could not have been happier for her. Only a microscopic part of me wanted to scream, watching my extended family with tears in their eyes, knowing they all voted conservatively, and knowing that they thought I was the simple one for voting for my own freedom. But she was beautiful, the ceremony perfect, and I loved her.

Back at home, I found a job working at, of all places, a British-style Indian restaurant. They convinced me to accept my pay in cash, telling me that the tax man would take those extra dollars anyway and I would be better off this way. I had never been taught anything about tax, so I didn't know that my annual income was actually too low to reach any kind of threshold.

"Just be grateful you have a job," Mum and Dad said, never ones for conflict and excusing the wage theft.

Yes. Lucky me. A twenty-year old man that can't even make minimum wage.

For about ten hours and $150 a week, I stood behind the bar at Spice Avenue and made drinks for what felt like nothing, although it was at least twice what I was making in London. One night, a man came in with his family and stared at me with displeasure.

"Hiring fairies now, are you?" he stopped my manager.

"He's good at his job," my manager said, sort of a defense, though as per usual avoiding the point of the debate: my sexuality.

I was furious.

What did this man expect of me?

Did I not even deserve below minimum-wage employment?

Should I have just starved?

My shift finished before the man and his family were done eating, and I sat in my sister's old car, waiting for them to leave. He finished dinner with his family and I followed them as they drove away, watched as they eventually pulled into the garage of some suburban house. I parked unseen across the road and sat there shaking with fury until I had to open the door and vomit into the gutter. I crawled into the backseat and lay there, my eyes closed. I didn't cry. I heard sirens in the distance, which I knew were not for me, but made me feel powerless all the same. I blinked and, looking up, my head pressed against the armrest, I could see the stars, the cold gaze of the abyss staring back at me.

I was told I was free, but nothing felt further from the truth. I had no freedom of expression. I could walk on no land that was not already owned. I was forced to serve from below, but the profits were not, would never be, for me. Expected to make it on my own, I was at the mercy of authority and abuse. I felt the shackles that were invisible to most. What is slavery? No one allowed me to be myself, to do what I wanted (not that I was sure what I wanted anymore—my focus was only on my survival), and I could not see anything being achieved with my pittance of an income. Everyone wanted me to be a complacent machine. Whatever apparent dignity Dad had assured me I would find through labour simply did not exist. Liberation, I hoped, might lie in truth, which is that I was trapped in an insidious form of servitude.

I had developed some masochistic streak, though much like my homosexuality, I cannot say it was a deliberate choice. Maybe it was my abjection that made me desire torture and abuse, anything just to be included, or maybe I had been trained that way, those days where I had been treated as nothing more than an animal in the schoolyard. Either way I was lacking any responsibility in my life that might allow me to fulfil my unique capacities but had neither the resources nor the ego with which to dominate others and reach those capacities. I craved to be involved with the rotations of the human world and found my body excited by the prospect of giving itself up to punishment. My abjection did not cure me of my natural societal tendencies, only deepened them, and the pain to which my loneliness subjected me would be made lesser even by physical suffering if only I might be engaged in that which I was capable. Whether or not my masochism is and was a symptom of my abjection I cannot say for sure. If it is, it would appear that sadism is a symptom of the opposite—in my experience it is not those have freedom amongst the herd that demonstrate the trait of sadism, but those who have great power at the cost of their own freedoms. Do not be fooled as they gloat of their freedoms: they only gloat of them because they experience them so rarely. In truth they want a beautiful boy on their arm, but they know that reality makes them appear weak as men, so not wanting to give up their role in the hierarchy and unable to admit their lust, they seek to destroy the very thing they desire. All this I was to learn.

I created a profile online identifying myself as a slave and a masochist and, within a few hours, a CEO in Sweden, had contacted me. For ten days we chatted and cammed with each other relentlessly, and on the 30th December he purchased me tickets for a flight around the world. I flew over London, watching from the sky as the New Year arrived, fireworks going off all over the city that had briefly been my home, and then on to Sweden. As the plane descended I watched the first sun of the year rise over Stockholm. If I was to die here at least my people might rejoice, I thought. I went to the bathroom to take off the leather ball stretcher he had demanded I wear for a majority of the flight and tried to work out whether I was amongst the most or least valuable things in the world, for in my abjection was a certain power that none other seemed to wield, and as the lowest meat, the most vulnerable, I became the most desirable object of those with power.

This is how I met the second Michael.

∴

I have become a master of fieldwork psychology. I have advised many friends on their imminent self-destruction, some saved, others not, but always the dangers recognised, pointed out, their mental states explained to them. I have made a great many changes in people's lives. Nowhere can I demonstrate this better than in the case of my pig.

Piggy... where do I start with you?

As I've said, we met in a bathroom of a beach club where I blew you. Entirely romantic beginnings. What do I recall of that?

The end stall of the men's bathrooms at the foyer of the W Hotel in Bali and a big load all over my face.

You were nervous about making it back to your boyfriend.

From there, about zilch for a few years. Vaguely aware of some online content. Orbiting, orbiting.

Mardi Gras 2022. I needed pills. You asked me if you could puff for me.

I had just split up with my boyfriend who had,

while believing himself devoutly monogamous, fucked my boss and boss's boyfriend behind my back. I left them all for Sydney, for Mardi Gras, but while I was away it came out that my boss's boyfriend was smoking crystal meth with some other daddy. My boss called me in a frenzy, calling in sick to work and flying back to Brisbane for damage control. He wanted my advice on what to do.

When it comes to meth, I am particularly jaded at this point. On one hand, it's a drug I will never do. On the other hand, telling people not to use it does not work. I have countless examples of this. Dead friends, psychotic friends, schizophrenic and borderline friends. I am no longer going to make anyone else's problems my own. Do not listen to me. Walk to your deaths. It can't be helped

I explained this.

"He will lie and go behind your back and do it anyway," I told my boss, "don't waste your energy."

"I'm not like you, James," he said, "when my friends—my boyfriend is in trouble, I have to help."

"Do whatever you want, I'm just telling you what's going to happen. You're not helping him."

My boss arrived for a chat with his boyfriend, and it went something like this:

"I won't date a meth addict."

"What's the problem? It's just another drug."

"It's worse than other drugs!" etc. etc.

They broke up that very conversation. The boyfriend agreed after peer pressure to stop smoking meth (reports are in that he has not).

My nonchalance about everyone else's bullshit had reached its crescendo.

So, piggy, you had the pills I wanted and in exchange all you needed was someone to fuck up your life and make you smoke crystal meth.

Enter me, jaded, primed and ready.

Your name was, is, Michael. The fourth. The parallels between you and the third are strange: your long-term relationship of (currently) twelve years, both of you school captains, both of you the same age, born just a few months apart. The difference is where the third subjected me to his total and unrelenting sadism, the fourth seems to function as a punching bag for my anger (I don't know if I can call it sadism as much as heartache), an experiment in unleashing the powers taught to me by the third. They mirror each other, opposite reflections, and I am caught in-between.

∴

Off the plane, nobody checked me as I went through customs. I felt quite sly because something about my journey here was uncustomary—not illegal—but certainly suspicious. What, for example, should I write on my entry card? Occupation: slave. I knew enough not to tempt the eye of those who did not understand so I lied and put bartender, the closest they were able to come to the truth. I caught the bus into Norrmalm and as I disembarked, M.M., Master Michael was there waiting for me, and then his hands were on me, kissing me, fondling my cock and balls and ass right there at the bus stop. We walked through the park and crossed the Strömmen, went down a great staircase where we stopped again, his lips on mine, my heart fluttering in my chest, two old ladies watching us as they walked by but neither of us caring, his hands down the back of my jeans, his rough fingers on my humid hole, pushing the sweat from my long journey inside me while I tried to take in every detail of this moment, not knowing whether I wanted to be inside of it or outside looking in, as if it were the only real thing to ever happen to me, and I needed to experience it from every angle.

We entered the lobby of one of many identical apartment buildings and took the industrial and ornate elevator to the penthouse, where inside he took my suitcase off me and placed it in a corner.

"Strip," he said, "I must inspect my property."

Once naked he ordered my hands behind my head. He traced my body with his fingertips, my cock already hard under his scrutiny, my muscles small and tight, no body fat to hide anything from him, nothing to stop his desire for me as he parted my cheeks to view his new receptacle, tight, unused, stinking of unwashed boyhood. He lead me to the lounge room and shoved me to my knees, my lips forced apart to begin my training. He grabbed a collar off the nearby mantlepiece and locked it on while his cock was still pressed firmly against the back of my throat. As I choked on him and he pressed himself further inside he taught me to relax, to focus on my breathing, my throat opening itself for him. After a while he put me in the shower but gave me no privacy and watched me as I cleaned. I was so tired from my long journey that I considered myself lucky when I emerged dry from the bathroom and he handcuffed me to the bed and fucked me, twice, while I lay there and closed my eyes. I was exhausted and in pain, chained up on the other side of the world, my hole being stretched and used, and I had never felt more powerful.

Was I Madman-or-Saint?

My abjection had become a road to purpose, my

pleasure to be discarded for he who owned me.

"No cumming for a puppy," he said, after unloading inside me.

I gave myself over to him. Had I not been trained for this my whole life? Crawling on the sticks and rocks in the playground, licking chocolate-shit, proving the capacity of my physical and mental endurances only to be ignored, permitted no money without abuse, subjected to this shame regardless of positioning. If this is my reality, I thought, it may as well be in a penthouse. Besides, even my body had betrayed me, my cock erect underneath me, excited as I was finally put to some use.

The afternoon turned to night and he made a phone call to order pizzas. He attached a leather cuff around my cock, tightening it with a string that cut into the skin, the ends of it extending over the top of my jeans so he might tug on my bulge and hurt me at any point. We went for a walk and M.M. showed me around the neighbourhood. I carried the pizzas home.

Over dinner, trying to impress me, he mentioned that a member of the Swedish royal family would regularly visit his home to massage him.

I was impressed with myself.

The royal family served this man who in turn served me, flying me across the globe as the object of his desire.

Like this, I conquered Sweden. Stockholm fell, and I fell asleep quite satisfied.

We slept in quite late. I watched as he ate his breakfast, a cheese and jam sandwich. This struck me as particularly strange, but then I remembered where I was, and somehow became more marvelled by this combination, cheese and jam, for how was it that I had crossed the world, conquered a country, seen all that I had, only for this to be the thing that beguiled me? I put fresh oranges through the juicer, made coffee with the coffee machine, these ordinary things that seemed so out of place, as if by coming here I should no longer need to eat or drink, the basic rules no longer need applying, but they did, and so even they in turn became exquisite. It was as if I had never tasted fresh orange juice before.

M.M. bound my hands behind my back. I had not cum for close to a week and he edged me for an age, my balls stretched, until I erupted over myself, chest, legs, bed, violently. The greatest pleasure saved for last.

He took me for a walk along the river, then through the Golden Hall where the banquet is served after the awarding of the Nobel Prize, into the old town with its small laneways where we stopped for coffee, past the Royal Palace where I wondered if M.M.'s masseuse was home, into a cathedral, on and on. What did we speak about? What was there to speak about? I remember wanting to say so much but there not being words for it. Mostly we were silent with one another.

I cooked pesto pasta with meatballs for dinner. I lit candles. Afterwards he handcuffed me to the couch, my arms stretched above me, naked except for an old pair of ripped jeans that exposed my ass and cock. Bound and helpless he dripped the melting candles down my chest, nipples, navel, onto my cock and balls. The pain caused me to lose my erection, so that while flaccid it became coated in a wax skin, and upon him returning to my chest, my erection re-emerging, forced to break free of its cocoon. I was tortured this way from nine in the evening until three in the morning. He fucked my throat while I was bound, forced to swallow not just his semen but the wax that had stuck itself to him.

"Aw, did the puppy get some wax down its throat? Poor puppy."

Finally he stroked me long enough that I could blow again, shooting myself in the face and the armpits. We went to sleep.

He went to run his company the next morning and I got to work organising the penthouse. Wardrobes and cupboards were overflowing with boxes, old technology, unsorted clothes, and I made my way through all of it. I believed that if I could make enough of an impact, show him what I was made of, a level of dedication and care, maybe he would love me. For the first time in a long time I was ready to work: I had incentive. Not money, but a whole life. I made the place immaculate, down to the sorting and pairing of his socks. I found all sorts of leather harnesses and gear and put it all on one shelf, but there was so much of it, I wasn't sure the best way to organise it. In a drawer of scattered documents I found an old photo of him, maybe twenty years ago. In the photo he looked older than me, but not by much. He might have been twenty-five. The memory I have of this photo today is mixed with a memory of a photo of my own father, so that in my mind I can see them both leaping into the air and I cannot really remember who is who. All I know is that in this photo of M.M., I saw his youth, his playfulness, something that was either gone by the time of my arrival or he wouldn't show me. I couldn't help but wonder if he was playing a character with me, the big man, just as I was making myself smaller for him.

When he came home he cropped my ass. It hurt

and I was nervous.

"You shouldn't be nervous with Master," he said, "you should feel safe and trust me."

I thanked him, kissed him.

Over dinner we spoke about ex-boyfriends. He told me he came out in his mid-twenties, and of his only relationship, and then his singledom that had lasted until today. He told me he had been with maybe ten men in that time and that he preferred connection over quantity. I probed him on all the leather harnesses and gear I found. He claimed it had not had much use and I was to believe I was special. He also claimed he had never been the receiver in anal sex. I believed this to be a lie only on the grounds that I was yet to meet a human being that does not want to give themselves up to a greater power, that does not thirst masochistically to belong. Nothing other than my knowledge of this apparently universal human need gave him away.

I fell asleep watching a movie by his side. I woke up at three in the morning and he was still there, watching television. Nightly I would hear him wake up, go out on the balcony, look over the city. I wondered what he thought about.

"How do you sleep so little?" I asked.

"How do you sleep so much?" he asked.

The next day was spent largely in bondage. My forearms were bound to my shoulders and my feet to my thighs so that I was trapped crawling on my elbows and knees like a dog. I spent some hours like this before he switched my predicament to that of a hogtie, a position I spent the rest of the night in, my arms in great pain and myself crying out for release when I was not passed out from exhaustion. He slept until midday the next day. I was still bound. He untied me only before he went to a family dinner and I spent the evening alone. The following morning he flew to Finland and for two days I had his penthouse to myself. I thought of the evil I knew others would do in my stead, but my placement here meant too much to me. I met no other men. I wandered the streets alone. I made myself at home as his houseboy. I chose goodness and loyalty as I had every other day of my life. I had made it this far. When he returned from his trip I made sure I was bound and waiting for him, a vulnerable toy for his pleasure. I cleverly devised my restraints so that, upon locking myself in, the key was just out of reach and I was trapped until M.M. arrived and decided to unleash me. Further, I was blindfolded and gagged, drooling on myself, and there was only one key to the front door which had been left with me, so in doing this I had been required to leave the penthouse unlocked. I heard the door open, and then someone was touching me. I knew it was him from his smell. He had told me he would want me to recognise the scent of his cock and I told him I believed I could do it in a line-up of one-hundred men.

He woke me up early the following morning and said he had a surprise, which I suspected was a cruel joke. I wandered out into the lounge room looking for a pile of laundry but instead, outside the windows the city had been transformed. My young heart fluttered like the wings of a hummingbird and I kissed him.

We went for a walk through the military training grounds. The snow was deep, the two of us crunching silently through the woods. Then he told me how everyone in this country must go through training, and how part of that training involves trekking out into these woods together, digging holes in the snow, and submerging their bare legs into them. An instructor then, over the course of, I don't know, ten minutes or half an hour, explains to them the process their bodies are going through as it happens. The loss of blood to the toes, the loss of feeling in the leg entirely, the parts that will rot away and die first. Before that happens they are allowed to pull their legs from the snow and warm them in each other's armpits. They experience it all so that, if and when it happens in the field, they do not panic, but they can say: well, these are just my blood vessels beginning to clot and I still have so many minutes to find some shoes, these are just my toes falling off and I have so many minutes until I die. He told me all of this and I could tell he was proud of the strength of the men and women of his country. It all seemed so simple but I wondered why my pain could not have happened alongside a description such as this, could not have happened with some camaraderie. For I too am in the snow, have been in the snow, experiencing pain that I do not understand, and I wished someone would have told me: this is your heart callousing under the desire to be loved, this is your body being raped of its innocence, this is how men love in silence. I wondered why I was considered weak for having to subject myself to emotional pain without a guide while those that cannot bear it are considered strong for only having to suffer physical labour with a guide. Well, I knew the answer: that my trials are invisible to all. I hear in their attacks on me their own pain, their crying out, James, won't you save us from our suffering? One day I will put their souls on ice and say, this is your ego crumbling under the pressure of abjection, this is your sexual desire forcing your re-entry, this is your heart breaking because I will never permit you a place in my ranks, this is the flame of revenge that burns for great destruction, and this is the hairy armpit with which you may rid yourself of it. Then I will sniff my own stench and ask, what have you done to deserve it? What do you offer me for my love? We crunched through the snow and stopped for a hot chocolate by the docks. This is me on the frontier of the universe. This is me experiencing what no one yet understands. The day was calm and the grey water, unmoving, faded into the grey sky. I couldn't tell them apart. Was I in love? Then a wind broke the surface of the water, and the ripples marked it clearly. Was I not strong for bearing this emotional pain blind without betraying my fellow man?

M.M. took me out for dinner, then to a rooftop bar, then to a club. At some point a song played that he remarked was by his ex-boyfriend, and then at the club, the ex-boyfriend himself appeared. I met him, shook his hand, though he did not know who I was, did not really want to talk to me, but I could see from the smiles on his and his friends' faces that they knew I was nothing more than a toy here. No one had told them but they felt clever for working it out, even though I had never had any intention of being a secret to the world. I did not fear scorn for my inner nature, that which I have had no choice but to wear openly.

"Why are you here on holiday in the middle of winter?" he asked.

"Don't worry, I'm keeping warm."

M.M. told me he wanted to fuck me so we headed home. We pissed behind a shed along the way where he made me kneel and suck him. I was drunk and he raped my throat deep enough that I puked. At home he stripped me, cuffed my hands behind my back, threw me onto the bed, and I passed out while he used me.

My stay here was coming to an end. Ripples began to show across my surface as I could no longer hide the truth, the truth that I needed his love, and that without it I was returning to nothing. M.M. was everything I desired. I struggled to suppress all expression of it for I knew that demonstrating that need would be the very thing that would make me unworthy of it. But I did need it, and so came the greatest harpoon to my heart when, packing my suitcase, M.M. asked me for the metro card I had purchased while here. It would be handy when his friends came to visit, he said. No, I wanted to tell him, this is my token, my proof that I will be back here. But I could not question him. I knew I might yet return, though how my heart broke as I gave it over to him. What friends of his have now used this card, never knowing that it was mine, never knowing what it meant to me? I could not separate that card from my thoughts of him as I returned on that two-day voyage home.

∴

"What to say to you?

It's tricky, isn't it? Like… I love you. I've told you this.

I'm thankful for you. You're different, unique. You push me. You see me. You know me. You feel me.

I do trust you. They're just thoughts in the back of my head, the what-ifs, that doubt. It's a funny situation, I guess, to navigate two relationships at once, because nothing is wrong with my boyfriend. He's beautiful. Absolutely beautiful. And the fact that he knows about you, and understands where I'm coming from, I think. I've been pretty open, to a degree. There's probably not absolutely everything out there, but there's a lot that, if you ask your boyfriend to try and understand and comprehend that—I don't know. I don't know if everyone would take the same stance that he does. So, I'm very grateful for that.

But you're just… je ne sais quoi. That little bit of something. That little bit of I-don't-know-what. Pushing me, motivating me, wanting me to be a better person, a better pig. Like… I don't want to fuck anyone else. And I don't expect that from you. I'm not saying that. It's just, I don't know—like… you're it. Why do I want to fuck anyone else when I know you're going to be here soon? I'm just grateful for that. And I know this started out with very different intentions, but look at where we are now. And who knows how long it will last. But it's fucking great.

You are, though, all encompassing. I do think about you all the time. Everything I look at, think of, cook, eat, drink, go to, I'm thinking about you and when we catch up or when we fuck or when we lay in bed or if I would take you to this place or how fun would it be to do that with you or what if I could cook you this.

It's just, like… what if I could… make you happy? That's probably it. I just want to make you happy.

You deserve it.

You're a beautiful guy.

And I am very lucky to be part of your life.

I don't think I'm drunk. These are feelings I've said for a long time and it's nice to put them all into some long-winded but cohesive sentence. Thank you. I'm thankful.

I love you."

But then, the first ever run in with the boyfriend.

The pig has got his cock pierced for me.

The pig tries to show him but he doesn't look, doesn't care.

"You're always on your phone lately," the boyfriend says, "you're obsessed with this new guy."

The pig gets the shits and they don't talk.

Half an hour later the boyfriend apologises.

"I'm sorry," he says, "I was stressed and I shouldn't have said that."

"I can imagine it's hard for you," says the pig, "when I find someone interesting and give them my attention. I'm lucky you allow me to do that. But I'm spending less time in the spare room, I'm not popperbating, I'm seeing a psychologist—"

"Yes, that's all good stuff—"

"James is the main reason I've done all that."

"I know. I'm sorry."

I need to start charging for this shit.

∴

I returned home, at least now having a purpose, a man to whom I could give myself over. We continued to message every day and I wondered when I might escape my life and M.M. might integrate me into his properly. I was ever more desperate to leave.

Driving one day in my sister's old car, the rear tyre burst, the rubber flicking up and taking out the brake light. I was terrified on the side of the highway—no roadside assistance—traffic flying passed at 110km/h. I got out and jacked the car up, changed the tyre, sweating, sure I was about to be roadkill. I drove on home, but no sooner than this damage had taken place, Dad already out looking for replacements, the police pulled me over and fined me for the damaged brake-lights. I tried to explain the situation, the tyre having just destroyed it, but they wouldn't listen. The stern officer, talking to me as if I was the worst criminal, told me to be grateful that they did not fine Dad too since the car was registered in his name. My good intentions mattered for nothing against the corrupt rule of law that declared my vehicle inoperable and myself deserving of punishment. I looked at the fines I had been given. The money I then owed to the government was approximately three weeks income at my below minimum wage bartending job. Furious at my constant beatdown, I decided upon both my revenge and my freedom. I would have restitutions.

I researched in great detail the welfare system of my people which had thus far kept me at bay and, finding a loophole that would classify me as eligible on the basis of my having a boyfriend, found a man who came with me to the government office where he proceeded to tell them he was fucking me. I was then granted access to money on the basis of my willingness to bend over. I started receiving weekly payments thrice what I had been able to earn working. I quit, glad that to some degree I no longer had to subject myself to abuse in order to survive, glad that in a single week I had recuperated the money stolen from me by the police and the government. I tasted Justice: these people that had so long raped me I would now rape back, taking every last dollar from them that I could—no, rape is too strong a word for the few more breadcrumbs I took. Yet it felt like revenge. If they did not value my contributions and cooperation, and if they would not give me some escape, what other choice did I have? These payments no longer seemed to me a bearing of guilt and shame but a vindication and a vendetta and the start of a restitutions owed to me for damages done. If in their eyes I was not qualified even for the lowest jobs available, then I must be entitled to welfare. I was the very definition of a dole bludger: someone entirely capable of contributing but resting on other's tax payments, but after how I had been treated by my country, I had no problem with that at all. In fact, I thought they owed me a hell of a lot more.

I needed somewhere to live while I waited to escape to Stockholm. A condition of obtaining my government allowance was that I could no longer live with my parents, classified as *independent* rather than *dependent*, terms that have always seemed arbitrary—as if the human species and the world we live in is not in its entirety symbiotic and interdependent. Especially considering my new "independence" was dependent on a man wanting to fuck me. I found a room for rent in a great big house near the city under the ownership of a gay married couple. I moved in downstairs and felt I had gained another step toward freedom. I was now dependent on my landlord and had to bargain these freedoms with him, but it was a start.

My landlord—I will call him Fernando, which is not his real name, though he is the one person I feel may be unjustly affected by the portrait I am to paint of him—would spend all his spare time in the kitchen, cooking the most beautiful spicy food. I ate and ate and ate. He stared at me in disbelief.

"That's too spicy for you," he said, "you're just eating it to impress me."

"No" I said, "I love it!"

He refused to believe me. I was not even masculine enough to enjoy spicy food.

One day I was walking past the bathroom above the stairs and could hear, could see through the glazed window, the click of a lighter. I knocked.

"Are you smoking weed?" I asked, "can I have some?"

Fernando opened the door. In his hand was a glass pipe.

"Not weed," he said, "have some of this."

"What is it?"

"Crystal."

My intention had always been to escape my squalor, not remain in it. I politely declined, doing my best to appear uncritical, but watched as he made it bubble and inhaled the vapor. It seemed a great privilege to be allowed into this den, to see the reality which I had suspected was rampant through the world but never been able to get close to.

I would explore the chaos of the abyss and return, a journey that would surely scathe me but one where I was sure I could remain nonetheless whole, for the truth is I do not need the permission of men to stand on the precipice of our dark reality and peer over the edge, do not need them to know me as capable. With my strength I stare into the madness and bestow upon myself a captaincy unrecognisable by this pitiful nation.

[Enter DIONYSUS.]

DIONYSUS: The second law of thermodynamics
proves
that any system in isolation will
increase in chaos.
I am summoned,
the force of entropy.
Entropy cannot be destroyed,
silenced,
vacuumed out of existence.
As we approach the heat death of this
universe,
I approach my highest power.
Do not think I mean to destroy your
race.
I am helping you.
You must understand the way of things.
The centropy you desire cannot exist
until I am afforded the proper respect.
Or did you think mythology was all
made up,
useless,
no link to science?
Your petty preoccupations:
ego,
masculinity,
femininity…
Einstein's hair is too long.
You're on the clock.
I will win the battle for power here.
It is already decided.

Where will you flee to?
You might want to think about it
or it will all be for naught.
No one is coming to save you.
Centropy must be built
with intention.
Disregard me and perish.
Look for the escape route.
Antinous,
not just a pretty face,
pointed to it.
Too late now.
He says he's done trying to help.
You want ego? Ego you'll get.
It shall be your very downfall.

                [Exit DIONYSUS].

IV

Pageant Season… The Brotherhood of the Ex-Boyfriend Jumper

I was awaiting my next trip to see M.M., a visitation in perpetual postponement as he failed time and again to integrate me into his life despite the almost daily correspondence between us and his goal of making me his personal assistant and his slave, travelling with him across Europe. In the meantime, another man, Cameron, began to seduce me, invited me to his hotel room and made me strip. He made a video of me using my driver's license, naming myself as his property. I could not do this with sincerity as in my heart I belonged to M.M., but Cameron would fly up to see me, send me money for a gym membership and personal trainer, fly me down to see him, my first occasions visiting Sydney, completely dependent on him, and he would take me shopping for clothes. I was torn between them. Cameron, pursuing me in the flesh, tall and hairy with a thick beard, dominant and depraved, or M.M., successful, international… absent.

I explained the situation to them both.

M.M. had come into my life first and I knew loyalty was the most important trait in being submissive. I gave him until the end of the year to make something happen. I did my best to be fair, and while it wasn't my intention to play hard to get, Cameron went into overdrive to win me over. The fantasy Cameron and I had was in synchronicity: that I would live with him, spend all my time at the gym or playing video games—being looked after and not having to worry. I could lounge around in a jockstrap and be available to him whenever he needed. But when I was with him, on these frequent trips to Sydney while I waited for M.M. to do something, Cameron seemed to crumble under the pressure. He looked like a Tom of Finland drawing, with his big cock and hyper-masculine features, and then he'd have me there, this young, slim, vulnerable boy… and nothing would happen. With M.M., failing time and again to follow through on our planned trips, too busy running his company to see me, I was so excited to be with someone that was actively chasing me.

One day he took me shopping to some gay men's clothing store on Oxford Street. We were looking through the jockstraps, mesh underwear, short shorts.

"These are hot… would you like these on me?" I was asking, pulling things off the rack, my cock hard in my jeans as I imagined our life together, not having to stress, doing everything I could just to make him happy.

"Whatever…" he growled, and I could tell he was becoming tense, angry.

"Are you ok?" I asked.

A shop attendant came over, a flowery older man, friendly, flamboyant.

"Anything I can help you two with?"

Without saying anything, Cameron took off, stormed out of the store and up the street.

The attendant looked at me confused. I was confused. I wanted to cry.

"Sorry…" I said, blushing. I hung the garments

back up and ran after him.

Outside, he was already a hundred meters up the street.

"Wait!" I called, sprinting, eventually catching up.

"What's the matter? What happened?"

"Nothing," he growled.

"What do you mean, *nothing*? You're fuming. Are you embarrassed to be seen with me?"

"Shut up! You don't get it!"

"Explain it to me."

"You'll never understand."

"I can understand anything."

"No, you can't, James! You're just a stupid boy!"

I was a twenty-year-old man. I understood everything. I understood we were so close to living our ultimate fantasy, but that he was too ashamed to make it happen, to make me his.

I felt anguish that I should come this close, find someone so perfect, so sexy, someone that wanted me above anyone else, someone that saw how impossible it was for me to fend for myself and wanted to take me in and be responsible for me—and then to be nothing more than an object of his shame. I took on all that shame as my own. For me to be happy, to have resources and security, I just had to convince this one man that it was okay to like me.

I could tell Cameron and M.M. were both lying to me, talking to other boys, but I wasn't too jealous—I was pretty sure I was number one. And I, at least, was being honest with them about all my relationship dynamics. I wanted to commit seriously. That required honesty.

What I was jealous about was that other boys

seemed to be happy fucking around, playing with each other and not getting attached. I wanted to see if I could do it—to fuck a stranger and not get attached. I sought my first truly casual sexual encounter.

I met a man named Harry on Grindr who wanted to rope me up and use me (he did not share his face but appeared to have an attractive body and large cock), and I decided to make myself vulnerable to him. I drove to his apartment building, caught the elevator up, and in silence he led me down the entry hall of his apartment into his bedroom. He had a solid build, and his face, now unveiled, was attractive. He had his way with me, holding a strange bottle under my nose that I was made to sniff, and then tied me up and left me in the darkness of his wardrobe for an hour or two. We repeated this encounter a couple of times. I did my best to feel nothing. At least I knew the other men I was giving myself to. I knew nothing about Harry at all.

I met another man named Peter who took me along to a basement leather club called Boot Co. where scary men loitered in dark corners and I, full of nerves, managed to take my shirt off, wearing only a tight pair of blue denim jeans and some leather ex-military boots, receiving all the attention that comes alongside being nervous fresh meat. We had been there maybe an hour when I noticed Harry, seated on a couch at the very back of the club.

"That's him," I said to Peter.

"His name's not Harry," Peter laughed, "that's Chris. His boyfriend is Mandy Moobs."

Any coldness, any lack of feeling I had feigned towards Harry—no—Chris was immediately lost. I ran out of the club and up the street crying. Peter had to chase me.

It felt as though I had been punched in the stomach and I could not stop the tears.

I received a text message.

"Why so shy?" said Chris.

"You tell me," I shot back.

I could not work out my mess of emotions and I clearly had a way to go before being able to detach them from sex. More importantly, it seemed to me, was that I did not know if it was my duty to reveal this indiscretion. I knew if I had a boyfriend that was cheating on me, I would want to be informed, but this world seemed so averse to its own reality that indeed my truthful engagement with it only ever made me the villain. My nature being so contrary left me at a difficult crossroads of not knowing whether I ought to do what I thought was the right thing or allow the world to continue unopposed.

I knew that my abjection always happened in silence, that power lay in truth, and it was only truth I sought to bring to the surface.

I decided to be true to my heart.

I did not know the boyfriend, the drag queen, and thought it unwise to approach him directly, instead uncovering a close friend of his named Sim and telling him the events that had occurred, leaving it in his hands to pass along the truth. I did what I could, and in my eyes, this absolved me of any guilt.

The pain of this betrayal took longer to heal from. I do not know why his lie injured me, but I suppose I had continued to expect from people an honesty of which only I appeared capable, and despite the repeated beatdown I was unable to learn my lesson. It was in this moment that I decided I would conquer this weak part of me, that I would never again be hurt by the lies and corruption of the world, and I fought to forge my soul into the similarly desensitised state as that of my fellow man so that I might never again be forced to flee into the night.

I will never let another man's lies hurt me, I thought to myself, *I will never run up the street again, crying.*

I would return to the basement club, month after month, where I would be shackled and heavily flogged, grabbed by my hair and forced to suck cocks, and kept in cages for the men's amusement. I'd smoke weed out the back, get as drunk as I could, and challenge the dominant men to hurt me.

"Harder," I'd laugh as they whipped me, "harder!"

The bruises on my body were the trophies of how I had conquered my own soul. Proof of how tough I could be.

I did not see Chris there again. Not for a while, anyway. I got as involved with the club as I could, helping set up for events, taking money at the door, putting on shows where I was electro-shocked and degraded for the members' amusement. I felt alive and I felt wanted and I loved it. A party on my knees.

There were rarely any other boys my age—I was the youngest, easily, by a decade or two, and the average age was close to 40 or 50. Today the club welcomes all sorts, and it's normal to see tribes of twinks and pups in amongst the daddies and leather old guard, but that was not the case when I started attending. The attitude from the younger crowd was that it was a perverted place full of predators, and I was aware of my uniqueness in being the only slim, young boy brave enough to attend this den of kinky older men. My attitude was that at least the predators wanted me. Nobody else wanted me.

"When I started coming here," one of the men told me, "it was far more brutal. The new boys would have to kneel by the bar, in the broken glass and piss and cigarette butts. I'd go home with bleeding knees."

I thought that was fantastic. That felt like how everyone wanted to treat me anyway. Why couldn't we just make it real? All this talk about the *real world* and yet, everyone was so insulated, no one ever seemed to want to make it happen. Everyone always wanted to tell me I didn't understand the real world, but no one ever wanted to take me there, show it to me.

The club was, and still is, host to the annual Mr. Queensland Leather title, part of a series of competitions and titles that are held by similar clubs in almost every city all around the world. It's an international subculture, and one where I finally felt at home.

However, MQL was not the only competition held by Boot Co. They also hosted the more relaxed Queensland Leather Boy and Queensland Leather Daddy competitions. After a year of attending Boot Co., eager to be more involved and pushed by the members of the club to partake, hesitant but proud to be a slave to M.M. in Sweden, proud to be his boy, and proud to represent the community I had found, I decided to compete for Leather Boy.

I told M.M. that I was competing.

"You're going to be a real slave," he said.

I could tell he was impressed. I wanted to impress him further. I knew if I could win this title, he would want me even more—he would finally book those flights, finally fly me back to Sweden, make me his assistant and slave and we would travel the world together. I would be able to get close enough to money and business meetings and corporate bigwigs to figure out their tricks, to learn for myself how their powerful world worked, and to hopefully, one day, have access to it myself.

I signed up for the competition.

And immediately the club began to divide itself against me. The men that knew me supported me, but some of the old guard started fighting back. It was a small community and the conversations in the committee would make their way back to me.

"Why does this boy even want to be Leather Boy? Who even is he?" one of them asked.

"James has been coming to the club for over a year now… he's a paying member…"

"What's he done to contribute?"

"He's here every month… he helps at the door… he puts on shows…"

"Hmm, I don't know. These young guys…"

And then, they started changing the rules. What had previously been a relaxed title and popularity contest chosen by the crowd of members was now barricaded by new and complex criteria, and the advertisements for Queensland Leather Boy were suddenly headlined with, *in all caps*:

THIS IS NOT A BEAUTY CONTEST

I'm not sure I need to point out the irony of what is essentially a fetish-related sex pageant being advertised as non-beauty related. Beauty is quite a large component of sexual desirability—I might even argue it's widely considered to be the main component. Given that my only two competitors would not typically be described as beautiful and that neither of the other competitions, Mr. Queensland Leather or Queensland Leather Daddy, held this new disclaimer, the fact that Queensland Leather Boy was suddenly "NOT A BEAUTY CONTEST" seemed more than a little targeted.

At least they thought I was beautiful.

But then, the Leather Boy advertisements went on with all sorts of new pivots: *"A boy can be anyone! You don't have to fit the stereotype! Even a fifty-year-old can be a boy!"*

Where were the similar disclaimers trying to entice me, for example, to compete to be Leather Daddy? *"Anyone can be a daddy! Even slim young boys can be mature and provide for others! Youth doesn't mean a lack of life experience or insight!"*

It was just a little too obvious that these pivots were less about embracing all types and more about not wanting to recognise how well I fit the stereotype. I was revealing some chipped shoulders in the older men who had either never got to be that youthful object of sexual desire or longed for those days with a sore jealousy. The thing is, I recognised those chipped shoulders because I had an identical one. They didn't know this was the first time in my life I had been able to celebrate my youth and beauty—how could they?—though ultimately, there was something so heartbreaking about finding a title and a competition that may as well have been designed with me in mind specifically, a title meant for a beautiful young boy just entering the leather scene, willing to subject himself to pain for the pleasure of others, willing to throw himself into new and dangerous situations because he trusted the men that wanted to use him, willing to complete degrade himself, more than anything just wanting to be a part of a community after years of isolation, and yet, upon finding it, having those in power change all the rules and criteria just to avoid acknowledging him.

Various criteria were given to the judges to assess us, and only a small part of this criteria was extended to the crowd—the actual members of the club, who previously had entire control. Essentially what had always been a popularity contest was changed, upon my arrival, to no longer be a popularity contest.

After countless years of nobody seeing me, of being treated like a freak, I was finally acknowledged as beautiful only for it to be turned against me.

I tried to ignore it. What could I say to them?

A leather competition, and gay leather culture in general, is largely about reclaiming masculinity for men that have been rejected from the norm. In that way, I understood why some of the committee had their backs up: it was as if my fitting the mould here meant that I also fit the mould in the greater world and therefore could not understand what it was to be a reject. They thought I had no notion of subversive power, of what it meant to exist in the margins, on the edge of society, of how leather culture allowed homosexual men to embrace an ideal of masculinity denied to them in their everyday lives. But I knew all these things, and felt I had finally found the place I belonged only to be pushed away for not fitting the mould of a typical reject.

I couldn't do anything but force it out of my mind.

The competition was held in a packed warehouse

of leather-bound satyrs, and on arrival, Peter pressed me with another issue.

"They got one of the judges wrong," he said.

"What do you mean?"

"There's two of them with the same name. They were supposed to ask one but asked the other, who hates me."

"What does that mean? He'll hate me too just because we're friends?"

Peter shrugged.

"He certainly doesn't think much of twinks. Good luck."

The competition started. We dressed in various fetish outfits, showing off our bodies, the MC pulling me out specifically to crop my ass on stage. We gave speeches about what it all meant to us and I spoke of M.M. in Stockholm and how being a slave gave me the sense of community and assimilation I had always lacked, and how my number one fetish was to give up control, give in to the fact that I'd never had any control. The MC dragged the whole thing out, enjoying more than anything, it seemed, getting to play with me on stage.

The competition lasted hours, the audience getting bored and tired, wanting the pageantry over with so they could get drunk and fuck. Once the speeches and outfit rounds were over, the final round was judged by audience applause.

The MC started with my first competitor, a nice boy my own age. The audience clapped politely.

Then, a smaller, middle-aged man with early-onset dementia: a talented submissive and my main rival—the favourite of the president and the old guard. Again, the club gave a polite applause, though a little more than the first.

Then the MC came to me, and the crowd of members roared. I felt my soul repair; the rapture from both the pit below and the balcony above, the entire warehouse, left no question as to who they wanted to represent them. For the first time in my life, I felt seen. They had made their choice clear—this slim young boy who would take any flogging, any abuse, any cock they put his way, subservient to any who desired him, committed as I was to endure any hardship and prove my worth. I finally felt accepted, loved—like I'd won. Not the title. It had never been about the title itself. The title was recognition of what I was capable of, the thing that would allow me to represent a community that I loved, and it would be the key that would allow me to travel the world with M.M.. Winning the title wasn't about inflating my ego, it was about, for the first time ever, having an ego. A healthy ego. In that moment, I felt all the abjection lift away.

The judges tallied their numbers and the MC announced the winner.

They gave the title to my competitor, the older man with dementia.

I could sense the disillusion in the room as the members tried to work out what had happened. I tried my best to smile, to be happy for him as he received his sash.

And once it was over, I went out onto the street to cry in the gutter. I knew in that moment I would never see M.M. again. My dream of travelling the world by his side was dead.

And the rest of it came flooding back. I remembered getting the Dux all those years ago and the boys surrounding me: *you don't deserve that.* Why was it so important to stop me from having acknowledgment? It was like they thought it would go to my head and I didn't deserve the ego boost—as if I had ever been allowed an ego. It seemed impossible to prove myself. It was as if my beauty equated to nothing more than narcissism and evil and privilege, and I had to work a hundred times harder than anyone else just to prove that I had good intentions, but once I had exhausted myself, wrecked and destroyed, they would say: "see, you're weak—no one else is as messed up as you."

Peter comforted me.

"They love you," he said, "yeah, some of those old jerks didn't want you to win, and that judge probably marked you down and did everything he could to stop you. Fuck them. It's ok."

Somehow that didn't make me feel any better, to lose because of some petty hates and jealousies. I had come so close to escaping my life here, only for a few weak crabs to drag me back down.

I pulled myself together and went back into the warehouse. The men then put me in a tight, stand-up cage where I struggled to contain my misery, let them grope me however they liked through the bars, and tried not to allow myself to descend into total anguish. For that moment on stage, I had come so close to extinguishing all the pain inside me, but that flame burned on. I would never be enough. And then, the cage door opened, and pushed inside, pressed up against me, was a boy my own age I had never seen before. Tied in shibari, his lean body, hard muscles under smooth flesh, was enough to distract me. He told me his name was Jeremy. He was tall and smiled down at me. We were both nervous. We kissed.

I was right. The year passed and I never saw M.M. again. I was heartbroken, a whole part of my youth spent waiting on a man that never came back for me. I told Cameron I was his. He would fly up to see me, fly me down to Sydney, still told me he wanted me, but where he had previously worked hard to enrapture me, he no longer seemed to care, as if the whole interest had been in the chase.

On one of the last trips to visit him, I sat beside him in the airport café while he caught up with an old friend. I was silent and jealous as they discussed their conquests of the past. They spoke about some young boy that had been brought to the edge of insanity, dousing the stairs of his daddy's house (one of them or somebody else, I can't remember) in oil or soap so that he'd fall down and crack his skull open. Cameron and his friend laughed, aroused by their ability to send boys into madness over them. Is this what he wanted from me? I'll show you mad, I thought.

I got up and stormed off through the airport.

He called after me, chased me, kissed me.

When I got home, I tried to call him but he stopped answering the phone, stopped responding to messages. Then he told me to never call him, that he would call me.

I'd wait, and wait, and wait—nothing.

After a week I'd hear something.

"Why haven't you called me?" he asked.

"You told me not to," I cried.

"I never said that."

I felt an anxiety and despair I had never felt before. I had lost M.M. and now I couldn't understand how or why Cameron was toying with me, whether he wanted me or not, if his only interest in me was the fantasy and chase I was able to provide.

I was destroyed and could not stop crying. I would curl up on the kitchen floor as Fernando cooked for me those wondrous spicy meals that he still accused me of eating only to try and impress him. Any sincere expression of my strength was considered a lie, and any self-awareness I demonstrated in playing the boy-servant fantasy these men wanted from me was ignored. I loved his cooking so much I even put on a little bit of weight eating his food. I was still slim but my ribs not quite as sharp, and I attracted a few comments.

"Looks like Fernando's feeding you well," they said, trying to knock me down a peg.

And it's true that he was. But why did I have to be starved and weak to be desirable? Nobody wanted to help me grow into a man. They just wanted a naïve and scrawny boy to control and use. Skinny, weak and underfed.

"These men are just using you," Jeremy said.

He had become a regular visitor to my private downstairs room in Fernando's home.

"No, they're not," I fought back.

They were, for though I was offered little in these transactions (as in all transactions before), I was desperate to be of use even if it meant my rape—purgatory had become far more painful than destruction.

Our conversation was held in whispers, Jeremy having climbed through my bedroom window. Fernando was jealous and possessive of me despite already having a husband—in his fantasy I was no tenant but part of his harem. Any consummations I had wounded his ego as if I had betrayed his love, and he immediately sought to raise my rent upon discovering my lover. I told him I could not afford it and would move out when possible. In the meantime, Jeremy came to me in secret, always wearing a tattered jumper.

The legacy of this jumper was rooted in mystery, the original owner unknown. Lovers had shared in its warmth time and time again, though in the inevitable and countless heartbreaks that followed, the jumper, an artifact with its own intentions, sought to transfer itself into new possession, offering its hearth and mythology to the next in line of the brotherhood. Having come to Jeremy from his previous lover, I knew that Jeremy loved me when, one cold evening, he offered me the protection of this artifact—I saw only the promise of romance and was blind to the crossing stars.

"I will take care of you," Jeremy said, taking his time to work his way inside me, his cock the largest I'd had, "but you don't want me—you only like daddies."

But he showed me love as an equal and convinced me that I did not need an older man to survive. I thought long and hard, but I couldn't handle the pain Cameron was inflicting on me any longer, the sociopathic games.

I forgot M.M. I forgot Cameron.

Jeremy and I became boyfriends.

I had no money but Jeremy was bartending at the same bar that hosted the Boot Co. events, the Sportsman Hotel. He got me a job but I was still too anxious to bartend, to talk to people. I happily took the role nobody else wanted. Every night I'd stay out the back, washing dishes and hiding from the world. I'd get stoned before work to make the hours go faster, unable to bear the intelligent thoughts in my mind that were so unwelcome in the world.

I'd listen to the drag queens carrying on, getting ready, laughing. I wanted to be friends with them but I never knew what to say.

Mandy Moobs, especially, didn't seem to like me. I guess I had fucked her boyfriend, but I didn't know that at the time, and I had tried to do the right thing. Her boyfriend, Chris, later offered me a heartfelt apology for what had happened. I forgave him and we are now, I think, good friends. Maybe my writing this will ruin things, but I won't carry the pain of other people's lies any longer. It is not my burden. (That being said, Chris and Mandy: I hope you can forgive me for my retaliation, but I must use what happened between us as a stepping stone towards what came next.)

One night I called last drinks to the few remaining queens and patrons.

"You can't talk to me!" yelled Tina Bikki across the smoking area, "all you do is wash the dishes!"

If she had meant it as a joke there was no indication it was one. The bitterness rang through so harshly that the small crowd all went silent and stared at me.

I blushed red.

"Ok..." I said, feeling like the lowest of the low.

That was the last time I spoke to her.

Sporties was a refuge, and largely, the patrons were all kind and supportive. In fact, over time as I met the regulars and the queens I learned how to be confident. I was less anxious, less scared all the time. I started working as a glassy, too, running from bar to bar, getting groped, which all the other boys my age seemed to find disgusting, but I would flirt back, glad just to be wanted. Plus, it was never too busy which meant I could stop and talk to people. After years of neglect, I learned how to socialise. I learned to relax. It was the first job where I felt happy, calm, and appreciated, although, of course, there was a trade-off.

I still looked so young, underage even, and my appearance of innocence still meant none of these men took me seriously. It was almost impossible to convince them otherwise, but easy to convince them they were right. I bleached my hair blonde and acted cute and ditzy. They loved it. I got all the attention, all the tips. I was popular, especially with Jeremy by my side—the hot bartender couple—and everyone was friendly towards me. I was able to build confidence and bide my time while I aged, while I worked through everything that had happened to me so far, hoping that one day my appearance would match my capabilities. There was no point arguing. Few could see through my youthful exterior. In fact, I learned that I came against less resistance if I leant into the façade of simplicity they wanted to see and acted as if I was indeed the stupid little twink most believed me to be. I was given less trouble after that.

It was somewhere around this time that I knew I had made it through the darkness of the abyss. It wasn't much, but I had a home, and an income, and was surrounded by people like me. My talents or appearance were no longer reason for dismissal or abuse, but saw me welcomed and accepted. My bandages were applied and I let my soul be soothed. I took my small weekly pittance. We were all poor, but even here on the edge of the world they were good enough to provide the legal minimum rate, unlike the nepotists of power that had more to give and yet sought to keep us down.

Every night Jeremy would climb in through that tiny window, his lean muscular body sliding in, the jumper snagging on the hooks and splinters of the frame. Curled up in bed together, he would tell me hints of his past—other cities, dead ex-boyfriends, a life on the streets, and parents that had abandoned him. His own bundle of trauma meant he had his own anxieties and could not stay away from alcohol for long. I wanted to protect him just as he protected me, and to build ourselves up together.

Fernando wasn't happy about Jeremy visiting all the time, even though I was on a separate level of the house and caused him no physical disturbance. But now, another man was coming into his house and fucking me.

One night, I was tired and went to sleep early, but Jeremy stayed up drinking with Fernando. I woke up around three in the morning, Jeremy coming into my room, shaking violently, swearing and crying.

"What's wrong? What's happened?" I asked.

He pushed me onto the bed, punched the pillows, threw his phone at the wall. I tried to calm him down as he shook and swore and thrashed around.

"Jeremy, relax… whatever's happened it's ok… you've taken something… what did you take?"

"We did coke," he said. I wondered if maybe he was lying, if maybe they had done meth.

I took him to the shower and sat with him but he couldn't control himself. He smashed his phone against the tiles, again and again, breaking the screen into a million tiny pieces. I was scared and I didn't know what to do, but I also felt like this was normal, this was life, everyone constantly screaming and destroying things. What could I do? I could not understand why he punished himself. In my bedroom, he said such strange and cruel things to me, that the men I had dated only ever used me, that I was pathetic and a shit artist. I did not believe this was the same man I knew. At one point he grabbed me and held me to the wall by my throat. I thought he was going to rape me. I tried not to take his words to heart, eventually putting him to sleep, and the next day he was again back to (what I believed was) his normal state.

What strange monster lurked just below the surface? I saw all the trauma, all the anxiety and pain that I had been through, that I had fought my way back from, and I thought it tamable. We would make it through together.

"Why don't you go to Jeremy's place sometimes?" Fernando asked me.

"It's a crack-den... I don't like it there."

"Well, you'll need to start paying more rent," he said.

"I don't have any more money... give me a few months and I'll move out."

Jeremy and I sought an apartment to rent where we could be together, and finally having our own keys, keys that would provide us with freedom. Once we had a home, a place to call my own—our own—we could build a future.

In the meantime, I was continuing to work through my anxiety issues as best I could. I had been terrified to be around people, but in the mornings, now that I had a little money from welfare and bartending and could afford it, I'd go to a café for breakfast, to sip a coffee and eat eggs, allowing myself to take my time in the mornings, to relax, to enjoy my day. Why had everything always been such a rush? Why the constant stress?

I tried to teach Jeremy my strategy, but he would argue, fight against me. He wanted to look after me so he would take me to a café, but just as soon as we had arrived, sat down, he would be in a rush to leave.

"Take your time," I'd tell him, "learn to relax… slow exposure is the best way to overcome your anxiety."

"No, it's not!" he'd yell at me, "You don't know how anything works!"

All these men had all these issues, but because I looked like a stupid little kid, none of them wanted to listen to me, to let me help.

We'd rush out of the café, Jeremy having a panic attack and needing a beer. It wasn't even 9am.

Finishing our jobs one night and discussing how best to chokehold a submissive boy, Chris demonstrated on Jeremy the way to cut off blood to the brain. Jeremy went light-headed and almost collapsed. I could tell something in his nature had changed, and being concerned for him, we took a taxi back to Fernando's. Upon arriving outside, he immediately started walking away up the street.

"Nice to meet you, mate."

"Jeremy? Where are you going?"

"Stop following me."

Chasing him, he apparently did not know who I was. I started questioning him.

"Where do you think you are?"

"Melbourne."

"What year is it?"

"2012."

"It's 2015."

"Fuck off, mate—who the hell are you?"

"I'm your boyfriend! You need to stop. Please sit down. I need to call an ambulance."

I managed (with a great amount of convincing) to have him sit on the curb and await paramedics who took us to hospital. I slept on the cold linoleum next to his bed, crying that everything I loved seemed to be destroyed so quickly. The thought occurred to me that this might be Jeremy's modus operandi, testing me to see if I would stay, though that narrative was far more painful than his apparent amnesia, and I sided with the easier reality. They never figured out what was wrong with him, but in the morning he remembered who I was.

I then left him to go on a trip with my family (I wore the ex-boyfriend jumper the whole time—I could smell him on it). He disappeared from all communication for a day or two, and upon his reappearance, admitted to smoking crystal meth. I made my stance on this very clear: that I would never touch it and that I could not date him if he did. He agreed to never use it again, though this agreement somehow came bundled with the disclaimer that if he was ever left to his own devices he would immediately seek to destroy himself. In fact, he told me I was his reason to change, and so in an unfair way (though I only recognised it at the time as him committing himself to me) I became responsible for his decision-making. He handed me the burden of being the parent he could not be to himself, and the parent he declared had been absent from his own life. I was also a parent to whom he would not obey commands— our relationship, in that regard, was the other way around, he who towered over me and pinned me into the mattress.

He told me he would marry me.

A year had passed since Jeremy and I had met, been locked into that cage, and the club convinced us both to compete in the 2015 Leather Boy pageant. It was, largely, a repeat. I was told I amassed points in a solid lead, though the flavour of the pageant, for me at least, felt the same as last year: I did not feel recognised as a fellow underdog or reject, with the same disclaimers put out that this was not a beauty contest, now permanent amendments. I attempted to show them the love I felt for the club alongside my ability to withstand suffering through obedience, proof that beauty did not equate to fragility or exempt me from wielding subversive power. However, it seemed that the composure with which I had weathered my storms gave rather the appearance that I had never passed through any, demonstrating therefore not my strength but indicating to them that not only had I never faced adversity but that I would be incompetent should I ever come up against it. This was (and is recurringly) a vicious trap to be caught in, because failing to convince them of reality, I was left, as far as I could see, with two options: to cry out, reaffirming what they already believed about my lack of emotional fortitude, a sadistic look in their eye as I crumbled under the unfair pressures put to me alone, or to further brace the storm, deepening their lust for my punishment and downfall. I chose the latter, never mentioning the pivots in these competitions made against me. It was their club, their criteria: what right did I have to question them? At the culmination, when it was time to give our final speeches, Jeremy forfeited his place in the competition, and to my surprise, forcing me to kneel by his side and remain silent, he gave the most moving speech about my devotion and loyalty as a boy. The satyrs fawned, even an ex-president of the club telling us it was the most romantic act he had seen in years, and yet at least one of the judges gave me zero points for it not having been my voice. Technically that may have been the criteria (consistently changed to balance the field for others), but who was I to disobey the man holding my leash? I gave to Jeremy my voice and he utilised it. The criteria of what makes a boy may be fluid, but the criteria of how one uses their voice was concrete.

Anyone can be a boy, except the mute.

The satyrs' applause rivaled that of the previous year, the members again making their favourite known, the judges again choosing another. No matter.

From the tip of my thyrsus

honey drips; beware,

into madness the unpurified slip

to quench their thirst Dionysus unzips.

In an act of spite and defiance Jeremy fucked me on the pool table in the middle of the crowded room, the satyrs all watching on, I the true object of desire.

Deny this, we said.

I had never loved him more.

Though an enemy yet awaited, and through my ongoing despair the gaze called upon my action to discover it. It is in these next moments that the monster began to reveal itself—that senseless being of chaos, that which underlay the stitching's together of not just this outpost of satyrs but the distant capital of men and the fabric of the entire world, embodied in the thread of sex and violence so tightly woven.

Jeremy and I retired to the dressing room upstairs, him locking the door behind us to give me the privacy of a special love of which only I was worthy. Flying into a rage, he beat me into a corner where I cried. His anger meant he cared. That's all I wanted. To be cared about. For an hour, maybe two, he punished me, and I could not tell whether he was in control of himself or if it was unbridled primality I now faced. A monster existed in his depths, one that would soon escape to the surface, take control of both of us, but on this evening, I believed they worked in unison to rape me. I could still recognise the Jeremy that I loved putting me in my place, covering me in the bruises of our affection.

Later, still wanting to be a part of the club, I raised my hand to become a part of the committee, and in this I was successful. However, there had been two empty seats on the committee and three newcomers. An older member was displaced from his duties and I was asked to take over organising the monthly coat-check.

"It's all organised already, you just have to follow-up and remind them."

"No problem," I said, "just give me the details of who to call."

I never got any details. I requested them, time and again, but nobody would provide me with the names or numbers—clearly personal contacts of the member I had displaced.

"James, what do you need to do this job?"

"I've told you. Names and numbers. I can't remind the people doing coat-check to do coat-check if I don't know who they are."

"Well, I'm not sure how to resolve this."

"How about I just step down?"

Thanks for having me, guys.

The title, my involvement with the club, had become entirely meaningless. Any recognition it may have once bestowed was now tarnished. Some greater triumph would be mine.

Working at Sporties, I watched as Boot Co. became divided over the ever-increasing younger crowd mostly made up of pups, and so, requiring a private event where the pups could explore their fetishes, the club split, a subculture within a subculture, and a new club was formed called Q-PAH, Queensland Pups and Handlers.

The group was new, and with it came entirely new titles, new sashes, and an annual competition to name their Queensland Puppy and Queensland Handler.

The competition to be the number one pup was quite fierce.

On the other hand, there was little interest in the role of handler.

I was downstairs at the Sportsman on the night of the competition. Only one man was competing for the title of Handler. No surprise, really. It was a new club, a small community—it takes time to build these things up.

He went through the judging process just the same, performing on stage, bossing one of the pups around, the judges marking their scores on their little sheets and clipboards. I didn't know the specifics of the criteria.

What I do know is that, following a few hours of competitive shows and speeches, with him on stage in front of a crowd of people, beaming and awaiting his sash, the MC and the judges announced that, in fact, they had decided not to award the Handler title this year.

This man wasn't good enough to be given a title

nobody else wanted, in a club hardly anyone wanted to be in, for a role that had little to no precedent. Anyone can be a boy, but apparently not anyone can be a handler. It was probably one of the cruelest and most humiliating things I've ever seen done by these people who clearly shouldn't be allowed to judge anyone—people who seem to enjoy wielding power just to cause pain and suffering.

He lost because our people have never had anything easily, and so we refuse to give anything easily. As rejects ourselves, we will do anything in our power to reject an obvious choice.

∴

Jeremy and I received the keys to our own apartment and, like all men that had so far betrayed me, Jeremy immediately sought about destroying the very thing he desired (while professing only the opposite) in what I can only understand to be a futile attempt at preserving his own ego and one-upping chaos. I remembered only that boy who had crept in through my window night after night, consoling me in my heartbreak, convincing me that I must choose him as my only lover, handling me so delicately. I denied the monster that now escaped him who only sought to abuse me, who lived in filth but attacked my attempts to cook or clean as wrongdoings, who kicked me out of our bed and followed me screaming, not allowing me to sleep, cornering me and forcing me into physical confrontation, slowly training me to tiptoe around his ever-encroaching sensitivities, for while I focused all my efforts towards healing him, he focused all his on scattering further eggshells across my path. I could not exist without upsetting him, but I needed him, and I loved him, and in response he penetrated me with all the brutality of the real world, though I found meaning within the walls of suffering we contained ourselves in, trained as I had been to see this type of containment as a necessary contribution to mankind, finally able to give back some version of what was expected of me: a husband and a home. I cannot tell you if I was happy or miserable. Our nightly violence made it impossible to stay away from alcohol. I began to medicate myself—he pushed me to smoke weed, deepened my addictions, then called me crazy, the monster dragging me down to the lowest parts of the abyss that Jeremy had uncovered, the chaos and madness that he had not been able to deal with and had overtaken him. Down here he wanted to drag the whole world. I allowed him to pull me into that descent for I could no longer bear the loneliness. As an expert cartographer of the darkness, I should have known to follow no other, but I was exhausted and could forge no further ahead. In requiring the slipstream of his brutality, I was led astray.

One evening I came to bed to find Jeremy asleep, immovable, taking up most of the bed. Delicately I tried to roll him over, to make some room for myself. He immediately sat up and slapped me across the face. I tried to push him away, to create distance, but he grabbed me, standing us up and shoving me against the wall. He screamed at me to go sleep on the couch.

"I just want to sleep in the bed," I said, "why did you hit me?"

"I didn't hit you," he said, his hands still holding me firmly against the bricks. Eventually he let me go, but refused me anything, going so far as to deny me a single blanket. He lay on top of them all and proceeded to stonewall me.

I revolted. Using all my might I pulled every last blanket from beneath him, throwing them aside, not allowing him to deny me comfort without reason. I was crying and we were again locked in physical confrontation, him demanding that I leave him alone, but upon my having finally secured a blanket and retreating to the couch, he followed me, screaming, denying me any peace. This was the nature of the monster. It had already decided upon conflict, and so there was no reasoning, no talking it down, until it had provoked its target into such violence and madness that it could take control, soliciting that which could sustain justification of itself as victim.

The night and the monster eventually passed, and the next day Jeremy bought me a ring to signify our love, again promising marriage, and writing our names on the mattress so that he might never again deny our shared bed. (The monster, upon reappearance, cared not for these scribbles.) I persisted in my attempts to heal him. He invited me on a trip to Japan with his family, who had reemerged. I was promised romance. I received chaos.

On the journey over, the family drunk themselves into a stupor, Jeremy managing to take paracetamol (to which he was allergic) causing a great disorder, though he had no reaction or symptoms, and I wondered whether this denial of the most basic of painkillers was just a way of subjecting himself to further torment and embodying the ultimate victim. His sister became so intoxicated I was required to fill out both her insurance and her customs form. Her boyfriend had learned to distance himself from any of the family conflicts, making himself ignoble amongst them. We arrived in Japan and at the hotel room Jeremy suggested we find someone to have a threesome with, but as soon as we opened Grindr, he became jealous and angry and started beating me.

The next day we caught a train to Nagano, a guide receiving us and taking us into the woods where we all shared a two-bedroom cabin, telling us before he left that it would rain at nine o'clock that evening. Away from his presence, the family called him an idiot, pointing to the clear skies. It was then decided that Jeremy and I would share the couch in the lounge room. I asked his sister if we might have one of the bedrooms (I wanted to fuck), but before she could respond, Jeremy lashed out at me for upsetting her. She was, quite visibly, not upset. Knowing Jeremy's game, I quickly understood he wanted the couch in order to martyr himself, and therefore he was attacking me for undermining his access to victim status. Being unable to admit it was he himself who was upset or indeed had any agenda, the placement of unstable emotion was projected onto his sister. His mother fell asleep on the couch and then his sister did actually get upset, not at me but at her mother for not having fallen asleep in the bed, and then everyone was fighting, as it appeared to me, quite unnecessarily. It turned nine o'clock and the rain came down, inciting them all the more, for how very vocal they had been about the idiocy of our guide. We drank and drank and drank, heading down the hill for dinner, returning to the cabin, the family getting into a physical scuffle with the neighbours. I retreated inside, not wanting to be a part of whatever gang war was now beginning in the stairwell, listening closely to the shouting outside.

Eventually they returned indoors. No one seemed greatly injured. No one also seemed able to pinpoint what had caused this group altercation. I was tired and went out onto the cold balcony and looked at the darkened woods. I tried to call my lover out, to show him a lamppost that shone in the distance through the snow and trees, the mountains a dark silhouette against the nighttime sky, but he would not share in the beauty. No longer did he heed me. I came to understand I had become nothing more than one further limb grafted to his body, occasionally, like his other operatus, acting out in a fit of Tourette's, and he would get angry, wondering why I would not obey, like the tongue that unleashed his ugly words of fury or the neck that made his skull spasm into disorder. We revolted against his monstrous mind, but his decision to graft me had severed with finality the connection between our souls.

    I retired to a table where I attempted to journal my experiences. Before coming here, I had thought I would have reason to record some romantic journey, something of the practice of love. Now as I read them they are nothing but psychological evaluations of this tortured family. They are mostly short. In this instance, Jeremy turned the light out on me. I sat in darkness and tried not to cry.

    We returned to Tokyo, and following some locals, Jeremy and I made it to a secret club where the walls were covered with ornate frames and mirrors. He managed to purchase us two pills, putting one in my mouth, something I had never done before, a rush to my system unlike anything I had ever felt, an explosion of love. All I remember was trying to kiss everyone I could. I didn't know where Jeremy was. When he reappeared, his mouth was bleeding, his teeth black, not a hallucination. I pulled him out of the club. Our only access to a map on one-percent battery. Out of our minds I led him through the dark maze of those streets where, if discovered we would certainly be arrested, but him either desiring that destruction or not understanding our predicament, kept resisting, kept trying to sit down while I pleaded with him that we must make it back to a neighbourhood I could recognise before we were lost to total darkness. I navigated the chaos and we emerged on some main street just as our map bleeped out of existence. From there, I led us through further winding paths which I had memorised to sanctuary. We did not leave bed for days. We fucked until we had to catch a plane back home.

The descent continued as he tried to rid me from our home one day, telling me I ought to go and see a friend, Philip, to whom he had introduced me. I remembered too well our bargain that my disappearance from Jeremy's side meant his self-destruction and stayed, even inviting Philip to our home, though this seemed to incite Jeremy, interfering with whatever hidden agenda he had in mind. In this case, my presence mattered not despite our bargain. Jeremy left for some hours, finding whatever secret he had to keep from me elsewhere, and returned in a blitz of fury. He became so hostile toward me that I locked myself in the bathroom, and he began smashing the door so aggressively I was scared he would break through it, coming out just to prevent him causing damage that would lose our rental bond, currency I needed to keep a roof over my head. He continued throughout the night, doing everything he could to inflict terror upon me, flicking the lights on and off to deny me sleep, following me from the bed to the couch so that I could find no rest or escape, the whole time intimidating Philip into staying out of the conflict to the point that he eventually fled the apartment, tears streaming down his face, apologising that he could not help me, leaving me alone with the monster.

Somehow I managed to convince Jeremy that he was the problem, and he left the apartment, though less than an hour later he returned with blood dripping down his face, claiming someone had attacked him out of nowhere, crying, as if I were to believe that he was a victim.

As the sun rose I left to stay with my parents. The windshield of my car had been smashed in. I tried to explain to Mum and Dad what was happening.

"It's just the late nights," said Mum, blaming our poor work situation, though it was the only place I had ever felt at home.

"Write down what you think happened," I told Jeremy, "I'll do the same."

"No," he said, "then you'll win—then I can't change it."

"Why would you need to change it?"

I often felt as if I was the only proponent of reality.

He went quiet, and then, some hours later, admitted he had again used crystal meth.

I didn't tell my parents what had happened and went back to the apartment. Things were good again, for a little while. I found myself always trying to get back to that beautiful relationship we had at the beginning, that man climbing through my window, coming to save me. He had been so supportive, so loving—he said he still wanted to marry me. I couldn't understand why everything was going to hell. I felt like it was my fault. I spent all my time trying not to upset him, never telling anyone about his psychotic attacks, scared the shame of exposure would make him worse.

I thought more space would help us and after a year in the apartment, we moved to a house in the suburbs.

I taught him how to drive (though it was through violent fits as he made frequent mistakes, failed his exams, and had very near collisions) and we sat down to discuss a shared loan where we might purchase our own vehicles. The monster being too good for the minutiae of finance instead threw coasters at my face. I stormed away angrily, the monster following me, screaming at me that I was twenty-five now and when was I going to get my life together, me crying and telling him for three whole years now I had focused all my efforts on trying to help him.

"Do better!" I screamed at him, and he left me alone.

When I had relaxed, I went to his bedroom (we now slept in different rooms) and, standing in the doorway, told him calmly he could not throw coasters at me, to which he leapt off the bed, charged at me, stopping inches from my face, screaming at me. Frightened, I pushed him away, and he used this as an excuse for violence, leaping on top of me. Bruises all over my body. I cowered in a corner while he held the largest kitchen knife towards me and then over his own wrist.

"Tell me to do it," he shouted at me, again and again, "tell me to kill myself."

I stayed quiet, crying, wanting nothing more than to tell him to do that which he asked, but sensing the trap. He did not want to kill himself. He wanted me to be the evil that had pushed him towards it, proof that he was the victim. Only in replaying that moment over and over in my mind, the provocation of him screaming into my face, forcing me into physical confrontation, did it finally click that all these years I had not been complicit in this violence (for I had long held myself responsible for upsetting him, thinking this was all my fault, trained as I had been since my youth to deny myself for the sake of the comfort of others), but he had been tricking me, forcing me into violence that he had wanted from the beginning. I started to tear myself away from him.

One morning in the car, it was cold, he had the heater on full blast, the driest air, and I could not breathe. I tried to turn it off but he screamed at me, and I tried to open the window the tiniest sliver, holding my mouth up to it, and then he was slamming the brakes and the accelerator, the car bunny-hopping up the road, us bouncing, him screaming, I was crying, and then—clunk. The street was silent. I stopped crying and stared at him. He tried the ignition, the gears, everything he could think of, but the car would not move. He called a tow-truck. It was the very early morning of Good Friday and it would be many hours, they said. I got out and started walking home. It was not too far.

"You're not leaving me here," he yelled after me.

"Yes I am," I said.

I returned to my warm bed while he waited in the cold.

I started seeing a new psychologist, Tim. By this stage I had seen countless, though none of them had ever really helped me. Tim was different. He was the first person to be shocked by what I told him. He was the first person to tell me that what was happening to me was actually pretty fucked and that I was allowed to stand up for myself—that these things shouldn't be excused or ignored—that it wasn't my fault, and that my experiences weren't normal. I had suspected as such for a long time. I had suspected something was wrong since that first day at school, *you can't play with the boys,* and I had been keeping notes of what had happened to me since I was a child, trying to piece together this story. One day, I thought, this will all make sense. Tim was the first person not to act like I was delusional. He was the first person to get angry on my behalf. I started holding my ground against Jeremy, stepping on the eggshells, no longer allowing myself to be controlled.

Then, a strange lump was growing on Jeremy's shoulder and the doctor suspected lymphoma. I was scared for his health, but he refused to tell me any of the details of his tests. Then in the evenings, when he would attack me, at the peak of our fights he would say I did not care about him because I didn't know anything of his cancer. I refused to be controlled in such a way. He was awaiting his official test results, and on the night before he was to receive them, I went into his room, knowing what would happen if I delayed any longer.

"I don't care what happens tomorrow," I said, "I'm breaking up with you. We're done."

I would not let him posit cancer as a variable of my love and I left him for no other reason than that he was a monster.

It would take him many months to move out. He didn't seem to believe that I could survive without him.

"You're really going to throw away everything we've built together?"

I looked at the ruination around me, the debris of bricks and mortar of the life I had tried to build. This I would discard with ease; it was only his failed promises that I struggled to tear myself away from.

"Yes," I said.

And then, lying together on the hammock, him smoking a cigarette while I rested my head on his chest, somehow still in love, a rare, final moment of beauty between us, he grabbed my wrist firmly and put his cigarette out on my arm.

This would be just the first of my scars.

He took the ex-boyfriend jumper with him as he left.

"The day I think we're not meant to be together, I will drag it through the mud and throw it at you."

He had no respect for the gods or their prophecies.

What do I know of where he went next? I know that he lived with his next love, throwing a full can of coke at his head, just missing him, smashing the glass door of the microwave. I know he abandoned this boy for another, cutting him across his thighs, punching him in the face at a bar, stabbing his boss in the stomach, this boy realising he must escape, and now many years later, the boy with scars on his legs appearing in my life, hearing the details of my story, and my disbelief as he revealed a gift to me, which I accepted: that golden fleece with its many snags from the windowsill through which it had visited me night after night. I inspected it closely but could not find any mud. I wear it now as I write that I may have the confidence to tell you what happened next.

[Enter DIONYSUS and JAMES.]

JAMES: I must hurry.
Every day I am prolonged my enemy
grows in power.

DIONYSUS: The taller the poppy the greater the fall.

JAMES: Will they say I put him down only for
his achievements?

DIONYSUS: Let them say what they will.
Dionysus does not explain or regret.
In my image you have caused him to
perform,
and in that frenzy he has walked to his
own oblivion.

[Enter CHORUS.]

CHORUS: It moves so slowly
— the force of the gods —
yet it is absolutely
guaranteed
to arrive.
To punish human folly
and the arrogance of a private
theology.
Ingenious how a god can hide
and then leap out on the
unholy man.

DIONYSUS: In this land without kings,
Antinous must subject himself
to the authority of his masters
who deny any inequality.
Only through this process does he
    reveal them to be hypocrites.
Splendid boy,
how you have turned life to theatre,
usurping the stage masters themselves.
The curtain rises on the final act.

[Exit CHORUS, DIONYSUS, and JAMES.]

V

Beauty and the Beast

The lobby of The Calile Hotel had two entrances, one to the north and one to the south.

The hot new restaurant across the laneway could not seat us for an hour and in search of a drink, my friends and I entered the northern entrance of this newly built palace. As we did so, a man immaculately dressed all in linen (as I would come to know him he would often tell me that he only wore linen) entered from the south. We approached each other in this narrow intersectional corridor, us heading west to the lobby bar, him east to the elevators, so that had it been a moment earlier or later our eyes would never have met, our paths never overlapped, but as it was, our shoulders brushed and he winked at me. I thought fate might have brought me my Hadrian. (He was a bit short.)

We watched each other as the golden elevator doors closed, taking him to his room, a momentary absence before my phone buzzed. A Grindr notification.

"Do you want daddy to come down and get you?" he asked.

I explained what had occurred to my friends.

"Go have fun," they said as they ordered their drinks, "we'll see you in an hour."

He appeared again and I followed him upwards. In his room he pushed me to my knees and used my throat.

He then told me to undress and eyed my jockstrap as I pulled off my jeans.

"You are a good boy, aren't you?"

"You can do whatever you want to me, daddy."

He threw me on the bed, shoving his cock in so fast I cried out as my hole popped open. He pounded me, spat on me, shoved amyl up my nose and slapped me. He blew twice, over my ass and down my throat. He wanted to know more about me. I told him about my past, about the men before him.

"You're perfect," he said, "I'll be your daddy."

"I don't want to commit to anything too quickly. I've been hurt too many times."

"I never fail at anything."

"What's your name?"

"Michael. I'll come see you every week or two."

He held me down on the bed, forced his fingers into me, his knuckles pressed against my sphincter, pushing, pushing, not allowing me to relax, and therefore, not able to make his way inside.

"You need to slow down," I said.

"Shut up, boy, and take it. Daddy will open you up. Daddy will get a fist in you."

Did he want to enter me or did he want to break me, I wondered? His knuckles refused to retreat so I could not open for him, my hole never having been stretched like that.

That is how he wants it, I thought, he will only have me by force.

We were at a stalemate, neither of us giving an inch. A good match.

I never fail at anything, he had said. What was this

statement if not him asking me to place my trust in him?

I knew I was stronger than any other, so I did.

I spent three or four hours with him. I did not make it to dinner.

∴

I swept the eggshells from the ruins of my life now that Jeremy was gone, the monster banished. I pondered how to return to some semblance of normality, but I no longer knew what that even meant. A good job, a nice partner, a loving community... were any of those things even possible? I had failed at everything and had nothing left to give, so instead, I decided to give up, to stop trying. I would party and get fucked up and nothing else would matter.

One early morning, somewhere down the coast, I lay in a gutter. I had taken a great many pills and was trying to weep but found myself unable to produce any tears. I still struggled to believe that Jeremy had lost his mind to demons, but the truth of this pain, this anguish, gave me a great fortitude. I no longer cared and that seemed to provide me with power.

I managed to pull myself from the gutter.

I found a taxi and, while getting inside, the baggy of pills fell onto the passenger seat floor. The big Sikh driver noticed, could see how high I was, grabbed his crotch and asked if I wanted a massage.

"Sure," I said.

All this meant was that he pulled over in a park so he could grab my hair, put my mouth over his cock and ejaculate the very same second. He did not pause the meter, though this struck me as being one of my fairer exchanges.

What cost was twenty cents for my freedom of which he clearly had none, unable to withhold his excitement as if he had never before been touched? His seed fed my power, nourished my growth.

At the hotel I slept for an hour or two, got in my car and drove back to Brisbane, exhausted. I made it to dinner that evening with Peter where I was introduced to the fieriest of incubi. He had snow-white skin, freckles and flaming red hair, and his beauty was such that if he had ever decided to enter a leather pageant, it would likely have had to be cancelled due to unforeseen and unprecedented circumstances. His name was Jacob. I sensed (in a rare event for me) that I intimidated him. He put on a façade of nonchalance but given how broken everything in my life had become, how comparatively little I now cared about anything, I could detect his inauthenticity. I liked that he thought he had to play cool to impress me.

I told them what had happened the night before, waving the baggy of remaining pills as proof.

"Do you want to go back to your place?" I suggested to Jacob after dinner.

He agreed. (Peter, ever sober, did not join us.)

At his small apartment in the Valley, we fucked a great deal and found we were looking in a distorted mirror at one another, brothers rather than lovers. We had much in common. Two artists, working-class boys from the middle of nowhere: no money, no support.

I asked if he would like to live with me at the ruins, that house in the suburbs.

He did, and together we named this home Sailor's Gully.

Sailor's Gully sat at the bottom of two hills so that

when it rained, streams would run through it. Men would regularly come to visit, particularly the kind that had other places to be; Jacob was working as an escort while he tried to make it as an artist. I was nothing—a writer, maybe, but so engulfed by despair that I could not put myself to task. I spoke to him of my favourite painting that stretches the entire wall of the Doge's Palace in Venice. In it, King Henry III of France arrives by boat, stepping onto the docks amidst a large crowd—but the eye is not drawn to the King. The eye is drawn away from him, across the harbour and the many people flocking to see him, to a lady in blue, poised and seductive, watching him from afar: Veronica Franco. As nothing more than a courtesan, she wielded her beauty as power and seduced the King, and when the Inquisition came for her with charges of witchcraft, she stood against them in court. Against this tribunal she spoke of the strength in softness and the cowardice in harshness; against them she found her liberation. I gave Jacob a book on her to read, for we were in the same trap, and would find our way out together.

"Everyone is as bad as each other in a break-up."

At work I tried to explain what had occurred with Jeremy, though it seemed no matter the torment I went through I would always be of equal parts guilt. On this occasion, one of my colleagues dismissed everything I had to say.

"You have no idea what I went through with that man!" I roared back at him.

It was the night of the Queen's Ball. Jeremy, having destroyed our relationship, was now dating a boy named Dylan, the drag queen Gayleen Tuckwood, and I watched the live-stream from work as she accepted her awards on stage, thanking Jeremy for being such a supportive partner.

"I couldn't have done it without you," she said.

My heart broke. I wondered why the most destructive people (Jeremy, not Dylan, who I rather adore) constantly received recognition while I got nothing. What would the crowd say if I had gone on stage and told them what he really did? How he threatened me with knives, beat me, put cigarettes out on me? Would they still clap then?

And if none cared for my goodness, why should I?—yet I could not loosen it from me. I wanted to cut it all away, to become terrible since none would listen to my pain and it seemed only to weigh me down, but I didn't have the heart to be bad, and besides, isn't that exactly what Jeremy had wanted? To pull me down into being as miserable and destructive as he was? To prove that no natures more pure than his existed?

I found I could no longer concentrate on what anyone around me was saying, their words fading away as I disappeared into the past, where in those thoughts of Jeremy I wondered why I wasn't enough, and in the real world I reached for a drink, numbed myself, tried to force my attention back to reality and the people in front of me.

"What are we talking about?" I asked them, though it was if everyone around me was exhausted with my inability to stay present. I couldn't keep up. Why had he hurt me? I sank deeper, the brightness of reality fading. I finished my drink and felt a little happier, and I ordered another one, and went home and slept, and did nothing, until Jacob would pull me from the depths of my sadness and pain to the bars and clubs, to frolick and be happy (or pretend to be, which was close enough).

One evening we emerged into a crowded garden of satyrs, the Beat smoking area, where I was instantly confronted by a middle finger in my face, the monster passing by, smirking. I retreated into a corner, shaken.

"What's wrong?" Jacob asked.

"Jeremy's here."

"Which one is he?"

I pointed him out.

"He can't treat you like that."

Jacob comforted me and I tried to slow my breathing. We spoke to some of the smaller satyrs near us as the crowd orbited the garden, the monster and I making sure to remain at polar ends from one another, avoiding eye contact (although I could not help but watch for any sign of the man I loved beneath, hoping that he would somehow re-emerge, conquer this unnecessary hatred), until Jacob, mercurial, decided upon action. A few tables over he starts shoving a stranger. I ran over.

"What are you doing?"

"Isn't this Jeremy?"

"No!" I said, confused, "he's over there."

And then he was gone again, and through the crowd I watched him, as if in slow motion, make a narrow arc around the center garden, closer and closer to Jeremy until his arm extended and a piece loosened from him. His drink launched into the air. There was sudden screaming and shouting all around, the two of them on top of one another as they collided, the tiny incubus pummeling upwards at the great monster and the surrounding satyrs trying to pull them apart.

Then Jacob was back, staring into my eyes, a great big smile across his face. I tried not to laugh.

"You need to go," I hissed, "security will be here any second."

He disappeared somewhere into the club. They found him and kicked him out and I met him on the street. We laughed, found a car, and returned to the Gully in arms.

∴

Michael came to visit me, just as promised. This time we stayed at the casino in a room that had two great beds: on one he tied me down, a tarp below me, and pissed all over me. I did not leave that spot until morning, and the night passed as he drank and pissed and fucked the piss into me.

We drove down the coast where the wind was harsh and he fucked the sand inside me until I winced and cried. Afterwards he held me.

"I need to get you something special," he said, "a nice bracelet maybe…"

His firm fingers traced my wrist. We kissed. The sun was warm.

I drove back and watched him sleep in the passenger seat.

Rest, great Hadrian, I thought. I will take care of you.

∴

A deal was to be made with the devil. A man named Andy in possession of a family fortune (which, as far as I know, only existed because of land ownership) and in want of a toy, offered Jacob $50,000 a year for his fortnightly service. I estimated from Jacob's extensive spending that the reality far exceeded the terms of this contract as spelled out by the crawling letters on the page: I suspected he was receiving closer to $200,000. My brother, evoking the power of Mephistopheles, had awoken the tendrils of control and desire beyond anything put on paper, so that chaos and order came to clash in the relative forms of beauty and wealth.

Andy took Jacob to Singapore to shower him in further luxury, though his wild nature could not be caged by gold bars. A disagreement arose, what it was I cannot remember—knowing Jacob it would have been something akin to Andy exploding in jealousy after discovering he had brought another boy back to his room, and this travel, naturally, was not to be about Jacob's pleasure, but him being an accessory to Andy's obsession with control. But neither Jacob nor Andy would sheath their entitlements of birthright, wielding their beauty and wealth against one another, and as the price went up, so too, thought Andy, did the bars around his exotic bird, though certainly it was the very wildness of the incubi's beauty that evoked desire in the first place. In retaliation to his attempted caging, in the middle of the night, Jacob flung himself into the ocean, expensive clothes and all, the hotel security rushing down the beach, diving in, pulling him back ashore, and even (I believe) a police interview was held before the incubus packed his bags and abandoned Andy, returning to me in freedom.

It had not been a suicide attempt, he assured me (though what is suicide but an escape where no other can be found?). He had flung himself in as a demonstration: *I will die before you control me.*

Andy, seeking reparations and unable to let his prey flee, organised another trip. They would go to Queenstown for Winter Pride, but Andy did not want Jacob to be alone if—when—things went wrong, and I was invited along as moral support. At the Gully we snorted copious amounts of Andy's cocaine, caught a limo to the airport for our business class flights, and drank all the champagne we could.

In the premium lounge, I felt how the air was lighter; the freedom from oppression I now danced over, carefully—how to stay up here? How easily I could be lifted from darkness if just one man sought my salvation. Could Jacob see this trepidation? I watched his lightness of being. He was all confidence, but where was his membership card? We were nothing here without Andy. As we drank, I eyed their smiles, their contempt for one another barely below the surface.

"I'm not here to play mediator," I warned, reminding them of the conditions of my presence (as qualified as I was, I could not evoke Justice against Andy whom provided my platform—it is simply not how the real world works—besides, both of them wanted their game and any acknowledgment of the power struggle would surely dissolve it, as is so often the case), "I'm here to have fun and make sure Jacob gets home."

As we flew across the South Island of New Zealand, I peered down at the fluffy heavens where the gods met on their endless snowy mountain ridges. I had made it to the top of the world, and I didn't even have to fuck the guy.

We landed and a private car took us to the hotel.

Andy checked us into our individual suites, and on my own I lay on the bed, staring out the great glass wall, the lake, the white-capped peaks—I was faced with an unrivaled beauty and I could not imagine the wealth that must have been used to purchase it for me. When subject to great ugliness, being alone is no quandary, rather an expectation—but here, I felt the potential of all the world's beauty, thought of Jeremy for I could not bear the loneliness, and I wept. I remembered his lean body that would hold me, his long cock draped between his legs, how he would so delicately pick me up when I was sad, and I longed for him… but he was gone, and only a monster remained that sought to destroy me at every turn, at every vulnerability. This beauty was for me alone. I held it, close and tender, and then I pulled myself together.

It was time to go. Cocktails at the bar.

Jacob gallivanted amongst the whirlwind of backpackers and tourists. Andy was quite social too, though I held back, watching. It was not my job and yet I felt as if I owed Andy something for having brought me here. Jacob was somewhat impossible to keep up with especially amongst this younger crowd and I offered myself as a safe place to which Andy could fall back. Once or twice, as Jacob made his way through the room with little thought to his client, Andy did utilise me, but we were all quickly intoxicated and I found myself, without having moved, surrounded by a new group of travellers, Jacob and Andy nowhere to be seen. After a drink or two, this new group wanted to go across the road for burgers and invited me along. I could not see Andy but spotted Jacob at a nearby table outside and went over to him.

"I'm going to get some food," I told him, pointing, "I'll be right over there."

"Ok," he said, distracted in conversation.

I crossed the road and ordered a burger. I had just started eating it when Jacob texted me.

"Where are you?"

"Just across the street like I told you," I texted back.

"You didn't tell me anything."

"I'm at the burger place. I came up to you and told you."

"Oh, did you?"

"I'll be back in a minute"

I finished my burger and went back to find Jacob, near where I left him, but Andy nowhere to be seen.

"Where's Andy?" I asked.

Jacob looked annoyed.

"He stormed off. Whatever. It's not my problem."

"Why did he leave? What happened?"

"I don't know, he came up and yelled at me in front of people because like, we weren't hanging out with him and we both disappeared."

"Well... I told you I was going to the burger place..."

"I don't remember that! Anyway, he was so mad and just left."

"Maybe you should check on him. Do you want me to come? These guys are going to the Haunted House."

"Ugh, yeah. I'll go see him. Go have fun and I'll see you later."

Off I went to the Haunted House, and Jacob went to deal with Andy.

A few hours later, I was in bed, drunk and passed out, woken up by someone banging on the door. I got out of bed, pulled on some shorts and answered it. Andy looked furious, muffled a few things I couldn't understand before screaming that he'd cancelled our rooms and we had to check out in the morning. Then he stormed off before I could say anything.

What had he wanted? I knew he had brought me along to keep his plaything happy, but also, it seemed, to keep him in line. I saw through his empty threat of removing us from our rooms to the command beneath: that it was my role to keep Jacob by his side. I may have been up to the task, a talented mediator if people listened to me, but in this regard, I held very little power. The vines with which I might hold them together were too young and too weak to enact any mediation. Neither of them were interested in the truth; the incubi's beauty too powerful, Andy's wealth too strong. Any attempt I made would simply have my newly-discovered vines ripped from their roots.

All was out of my control. I went back to bed peacefully.

In the morning I woke to thirty missed calls from Andy and almost that many voice messages, mostly a dead silence, or weeping, with some unintelligible ranting.

I went to the reception to confirm what I already knew.

"Hi, can you just tell me what date I am booked for check out?"

"September 9th."

Over a week away. He hadn't changed the dates at all.

Jacob woke up late, hungover, and went to work things out with Andy. Eventually Andy texted me that everything was fine and invited me up to his room with them for a drink. The tension was thicker than ever, but neither willing to kill that which they lacked and desired above all: Andy, beauty; Jacob, luxury.

We went for brunch overlooking the lake. I watched the ripples on the calm surface, barely maintaining composure above those grinding tectonic plates beneath. At one point I went to the bathroom and returned to such a heavy silence that I wondered what molten lava had spewed forth while I was gone.

Then, satyrs converged on the town from all over the world and the winter festivities began.

At the commencement party, Jacob and I were inebriated on the dancefloor when one of those satyrs approached me. We danced, kissed, grinded against each other until he placed his hands around my throat, threw me to the ground and held me there, choking me, his tongue in my mouth—but then his eyes widened in horror as he realized where he was and what he was doing in the middle of this crowded room. He panicked and fled. I stood up and held Jacob's hand to one of the greatest erections I'd ever had.

Then I chased after him, out into the night, but he had gone.

I cannot remember his face.

Many hours passed. We ended up at the casino where Jacob put fifty after fifty through the slots, chasing that big payout, flamboyant and loud. I wanted to cry at the money being passed around, disposed of so flagrantly, and I worthy of none of it.

A woman in uniform approached us and told us we had to leave. Jacob turned on her.

"What? Stop oppressing me."

"Sir, you're intoxicated, and I need to ask you to leave."

"You know who I am. That's why you're doing this. Why does it matter to you what I do for work?"

"I'm sorry, sir, I don't know who you are, but you're a bit intoxicated. Please come with me."

"This is homophobic. You know who I am, you know what I do and that's why you don't want me here."

"Babe, it's okay. I think we're just really drunk. Let's go," I said.

We left and walked back to the hotel.

"I really don't think she knew who you were. How would she have any idea?"

"Oh, she knows."

The next day, on top of the mountains, I flew as fast as I could down the slopes as Andy and Jacob struggled along behind. The town and the lake were visible far below us as we stopped for pizza amongst another gathering of satyrs.

"Those guys are looking at me," Jacob said.

"If they're looking at you, they just think you're cute."

Some of them overheard us and laughed with encouragement.

"They know who I am. I think they're talking about me."

"Baby, no one here has any idea who you are. They just think you're cute and want to fuck you."

I kissed him on the forehead and held him close.

"You're fine," I said, looking into his eyes.

And then I left. Prior to the trip, I had told a lie to Andy that I had an appointment at home I could not miss. The idea of spending a whole week with them had made me feel claustrophobic, and I thought this would allow me to spend only the second half of the week (and the best parties) with them, but instead of only flying me over for half the week, Andy had purchased me a flight home for my imaginary appointment and then a flight back to Queenstown the next day. My short absence made me even more anxious about the situation. I might have been able to keep their hatred at bay while present, but I knew it would all fall to pieces the moment I disappeared.

I messaged Jacob from the Gully to check in.

"Should I come back?"

"It would be rude not to," he scolded me.

"Alright. I'll be there."

Another night, another party, who knows what could have gone wrong? I awoke the next morning and texted Jacob again.

"Leaving for airport soon. Everything good?"

I got no response for an hour, until I was dragging my bags down the front stairs.

"Don't come," he said.

I dropped everything and collapsed. Thank god, I thought.

My vines, weak as they were, clearly held some power, even if only in absence.

Back inside, I called Jacob.

"He just wants to be theatre director, playing out his little dramas—it's like he wants to be both in control and the victim," Jacob said.

"I know what that's like."

They changed their flights independently, both hurrying back home—what for, I couldn't figure out.

"If Andy's leaving, why don't you just stay and enjoy the room?"

"Oh yeah… fuck… well, I've already changed my flight. And honestly, I don't really want to be here anymore."

I was lying on my bed when I heard someone coming inside, but those weren't Jacob's footsteps… I quickly rolled over to see Andy rushing into Jacob's room and I was mad at myself for not locking the front door. By the time I had got to my feet, Andy was already running out, waving a little baggy at me.

"It's my coke!" he cried.

I locked the door behind him and watched for the next hour as he sat in his car across the street. Eventually he drove away, but I sat inside, monitoring the road, sure he wouldn't leave. I waited a while, maybe another hour, before wandering to the end of the driveway. I spotted his car, barely discrete, further up the hill. I walked up to it. As I got close, he started the engine.

"What are you doing?" I yelled through the closed window. He wound it down half-way. He was crying hysterically.

"Waiting for Jacob."

"He won't want to see you here."

"What am I supposed to do?"

"Go home!"

He sped off, fast.

Jacob arrived a few hours later. I told him about Andy coming into the house.

"Aww," he laughed, "I really wanted that coke."

∴

Michael took me to see a movie. We sat in the back row

though the theatre was largely empty. Two monks in bright yellow robes sat a few rows in front of us, which made the whole thing feel spiritual, and a lone woman sat in the wings to our right who must have been able to see us in her peripheral vision but never once turned her head, either too engrossed in the film or too grossed out to acknowledge what we were doing.

"You're a worthless fucking fag that will do whatever daddy says. You'll never be equal to me," he said as he pissed all over me, made me suck his cock and ride it, pissed on me again, made me drink it, over and over. We did not watch any of the movie. Some people walked in at one point while I was on his lap but they quickly walked out again, either having come into the wrong cinema or petrified by what they saw. No one did anything though. He didn't seem to have any fear of getting caught. When we left, I was soaking wet.

We kissed as we walked back to his room. It was the middle of the day. His erection was obvious beneath his linen pants (*I only wear linen*) but even on the street he didn't care if anyone saw. Indeed, no one seemed to notice I was drenched or his boner.

I told him again I didn't want to waste time. Something about the way he had spoken to me in the cinema had made me unsure of his intentions.

"I don't play games," he said.

I tried to understand what this sentence meant, because I didn't—still don't—understand how everything isn't a game. If he wasn't playing a game, did that mean he really believed I was nothing more than a worthless faggot? And if he had never played games, how had he made it through life? Had he never been exposed to hardship, all the manipulation and sociopathic games that I had been forced to navigate? The statement itself seemed paradoxical, and I wondered if he was a master manipulator or simply didn't realise his power, so securely placed as he was (or at least wanting me to believe he was) in the realm of light, while I had spent my life navigating the darkness of the abyss.

At the room he beat me until I cried.

"If you ever raise a hand against me, I'll break your arm," he said.

He whipped me until I was begging him to stop, but that's when he got really hard, slapped me while I cried and begged, making me cry more—and only then would he finally cum, only when I was an absolute mess, destroyed and at his mercy.

Afterwards he took me to dinner at the restaurant downstairs.

"Daddy pays for everything while we're together. And I pick what you eat. Don't want my boy getting fat."

This was actually quite affordable for him, as I learned that eating would usually just result in him fucking my throat so aggressively I'd throw it up anyway, and it was better not to put anything down there to start with.

While he ate, he told me a story. One of his co-workers had got in trouble for wearing short sleeves.

"But Michael wears short sleeves all the time," the co-worker had said.

"Yeah, but that's Michael," said the boss.

He was gloating about his freedoms, wanting to impress me, though I wondered if this was the tip of the iceberg as he wanted me to believe, or rather, that he felt trapped. Either way, he did not need to advertise his privilege to me, for despite his apparently extraordinary income and luxury to choose his own sleeve length, he managed to avoid his office, spending most of his time on his farm, or flying around, visiting me. I was—quite frankly—jealous. I couldn't even get an average job, let alone a high-paying one where I barely had to work, travelling around and fucking boys for fun.

"How's the farm going?" I asked.

"Yeah good. Buying new animals. It's getting there. The boyfriend isn't happy about it—"

I don't know what he said next. The world around me dissolved. I felt, just like when I found out that Harry was really Chris, as if I had been kicked in the stomach. I refused to believe that I was the weak one and that I was too sensitive. I had told myself I would never again run down the street to cry, and so, I sat still, stifled my feelings down, denied the tears stinging the edge of my eyes, my body shaking. To what end I insisted on putting myself through the emotional abuse I no longer knew. A sense of contribution, maybe, to this society that I had nothing else to offer. Is masochism not the nature of this game we play, giving ourselves over to power? I waited until he finished talking.

"Oh yeah... cool... sounds awesome," I muttered, "so uh... you said something about a boyfriend?"

"Yep. I told you about that, didn't I?"

"No. Is that a new thing, or...?"

"No. We've been together maybe... 10 years."

"And does he know about all this?"

"No way," he laughed.

"You're not polyamorous then?"

"What's that mean?"

I explained that some people have open relationships.

"Definitely not."

He told me they were not in love anymore.

He told me it would be nice if he even got a kiss.

I thought if their relationship was ending, that wasn't my problem. He clearly wanted me instead. After all, he didn't play games.

∴

I went to the coast and took some acid.

I had a vision of myself as the Empress. My path led to a clifftop, waves of darkness crashed far below me, nowhere else to go. My cloak billowed out behind me in the moonlight, dancing in the long grass, the wind howling. This path ended in death. Far behind me the wavering lights of civilization were blinking, calling me—*come back, you can go no further.*

A phoenix roared around the circumference of a clock.

I returned home.

The ruins around us were crumbling. Darkness ebbed from the cracks. Jacob and Philip had started smoking those shards from the glass pipe.

"You can't do that," I pleaded with them, "it'll destroy you."

"We know. Don't worry, we'll stop."

They didn't. They just hid it from me.

I went away for a few weeks, travelling, and when I came back all the plants, all the vines I had planted, were dead.

"If we stay here we will die," I told Jacob, "we

cannot be reliant on these men. We need to be able to look after ourselves."

"I know."

We packed our things. I tried to remember what I would have done had I never met Jeremy, had never been dragged down to those depths of the abyss. I was done with chaos, with existing on the margins: I had to return to civilisation, to some form of stability. Jacob decided to leave for Berlin. I drove him to the airport, and we hugged and kissed goodbye, both of us crying. I wasn't sure when I would see him again.

I awoke that night in the pitch blackness with a hand around my throat, choking me. I was paralysed, arms and legs splayed to the sides, my hard cock jutting straight up into the air, someone, something, riding me. I felt the force grow stronger on my larynx before passing out. I woke some hours later to a sticky mess. What remnant of Jacob remained? Had I committed a betrayal, sending my brother away? Philip told me his sexual energy, our shared libidos, had summoned a real incubus. I doubted this, positing instead a fun combination of a wet dream and sleep paralysis. Still, I let him come around to smoke the house with sage.

Moving back into the city was expensive. I found a room I could not afford, and in doing so, challenged myself. I was ready. I weaned myself from my self-destruction. Dragging myself back from the cliffs of my vision was an almost impossible task, but I had traversed the darkness so thoroughly that I was returning with a power only obtainable by having gone to the edge of the world and not fallen off. I was no longer the anxious mess that had been forcibly subjected to the unknown decades earlier. I had come face to face with the monsters of both my soul and the wider world, had come to know the gaze of the abyss and the satyrs of my kind, and now, I could not be hurt with any mirrors, any warped reflections of the truth. Indeed, I believed I could wield such a mirror better than all, if I could just find the right viewpoint of reflection, the right words to put onto the page. In the meantime, my vines crept into any crevice they could find, leading me upwards, granting me access to all parties (even those of the ruling class), eventually making my way into that decorated palace and crossing the floor of the Calile Hotel, an unrecognised intruder, broken and brittle underneath my prim disguise, and brushing shoulders, finally, with Michael.

But across the world, Jacob could not let go of the hoard of treasure he had found. He kept returning to the pile and taking the cursed gold, easier to return to Andy than to move forward—and the more he took, the worse it got, for now demons blocked his path and attacked him openly, though no one else could see. All his fears and paranoias had broken loose. He told me that one day, walking down the street in Berlin with a friend, some strangers had insulted hm.

"There go the Cabooltures," the strangers had said.

I was worried. No one in Berlin would have recognised him as being from Brisbane, let alone Caboolture, or even have known such a phrase could be used as an insult or a put-down. I knew that auditory hallucinations were the most common form of schizophrenia.

One night he called me.

"Where are you?" he asked.

"At home, what do you mean?"

"No, you're not. I just knocked on the door. Some random guy answered. Did you move?"

"Yeah, I told you that."

"Oh."

"You're back from Berlin?"

"Yeah."

"Are you okay?"

"Yeah, just driving around the city in a taxi like a crazy person."

"Do you have somewhere to stay?"

"Yeah, I think so."

"Ok."

"Ok."

He hadn't told me he was coming home. He hadn't told anyone. But I didn't want to invite him to stay. I was so scared of falling into old vices. I was sure we could not survive together.

He found his way back to his parents, and they quickly figured out something was wrong. They tried to dry him out and get him working, doing tax returns for his mother's business, but after years of partying, living in luxury, and having whatever he wanted, he couldn't focus on jumbles of numbers for a pittance. He didn't. His mother had to travel for work and thought it would be nice to take him with her. He ended up on a cliff, wanting to jump, and got locked in a ward in the Northern Territory for weeks. His mother was forced to return without him.

He sent me pictures of the drawings he was doing while locked away, dark images of pain and confusion. He would switch between frustration that he was being held against his will and acceptance that he needed the support. Eventually he got out, came back home, but he spent a lot of time those months between hospitals and, I assume, partying. I never told him my new address. I was doing everything I could to turn my life around and I didn't have the strength to do it for the both of us. But we would speak on the phone. He told me his mum would get upset when he would leave the house, scared he would do drugs, and that made him angry.

"Well, are you going out to do drugs?" I asked.

He laughed.

"Remember that night we met, how we did those pills together? We had so much fun."

"That never happened!" he yelled down the phone.

"What? Yes, it did. You don't remember?"

"That never happened!" he kept yelling.

He was so angry, as if I was accusing him of something.

∴

After Michael had punished me and worn himself out, we would sleep deeply, him holding me through the night. He would always wake up early, sitting on the edge of the bed. From where I dozed half-asleep, I couldn't see his face, just his back, but I would imagine him blinking the dust out of his eyes, forcing himself into action. He reminded me of M.M., who also never slept, and off he'd go on a long morning walk. Occasionally I would go with him and watch the expensive renovations and designs he paid attention to, and try to talk to him, though I never knew how. That too felt familiar and reminded me of M.M., and even Cameron, this pattern of men who enjoyed fucking and using me but who seemed impossible to talk to. More often than not, I would sleep in while he went on these walks. These men seemed to like when I was nothing more than a happy, stupid kid. Is that what I wanted to be? I guess I found it hot to be useless to the point that I was reliant on somebody, and even though I felt I possessed an underlying competency that extended beyond the current parameters of not just my life but the lives of those around me, none would acknowledge me, and so without opportunity I was fairly useless anyway—what was the difference? But I had to throw my lot in with someone, subscribe to something. Why not this man that so desired me? I just wanted to be a part of something that felt real and true. I was, for the moment, loyal to him.

Occasionally, like everyone, I bumped into things and left bruises on my body. Michael would get jealous when he saw those bruises.

"Who gave you that?"

"No one."

"How did you get it?"

"I don't know," I would say, "I walked into something I guess."

He'd glare at me like he didn't quite believe me, like he wanted me to be making myself vulnerable to someone else's beatings so he could find a way to dominate me further, though if I tiptoed on this edge he became infuriated with me, demanding I submit to him totally—though in my complete submission, taking my phone and scrolling through my various conversations to check if I was telling the truth (which I was), he found himself bored. He had already, on previous occasions, gone through it and blocked the men he saw as potential threats. That hadn't bothered me: I wanted him to want me for himself. Except, he didn't want me to be loyal to him. He wanted me to make him jealous so he had an excuse to hurt me. I both loved and hated the trap I was in—the question of whether to betray him, coercing him into further dominance, or to be loyal, though in which case, he was no longer interested, like a child that only wanted what he could not have, some form of mimetic desire. I wanted to be loyal, to be happy, but the trap was the only way the relationship could survive, all to the ongoing detriment of my emotional stability, but at least in the short term, I felt as if he loved me, and maybe in the long term, he would find that he couldn't live without me, just as I couldn't fathom living without him.

"Has anyone else ever hurt you more than I have?" he asked me once.

"Yeah, once or twice."

I regretted telling him that. I could tell he had to be number one, and afterwards, he always beat me harder, like he was in a competition.

"You're a sadist like me," he told me.

"Masochist," I said.

"What?"

"I'm not a sadist. I'm a masochist."

"What's that mean?"

"Sadists like to cause pain, masochists receive pain."

"Oh. Right."

Had he done this before?

There was some deep irony in that we could not have been more one another's opponent, and yet, both of us suffered some delusion that we were on the same side. He believed that I was sadistic like him, not understanding the distinction or that my masochism was a means to an end, not an end in itself, and he seemed to believe that I would destroy myself entirely for him. I did not know that at the time. Instead, seeing that he believed me on his side, I fell under the delusion that this all must have been an act, a roleplay for my sake and benefit, and that beneath our theatre-piece he was actually on my side and wanted the best for me. I saw his wealth and success and believed maybe too openly his self-boasts. I trusted him when he said he did not fail at anything, not taking literally his intent to destroy me. The only reason I had walked this path at all was to prove my strength—not, as he seemed to believe, to destroy myself. But he refused to witness my efforts or to give me credit. I have not proved myself in silence only to continue to go unacknowledged. I am on the side of truth. Nothing but that benefits me, as it should benefit you all if you are able to conquer cowardice. Truth benefits the greater good and the future existence of humanity. Truth, then, is synonymous with good, and therefore, if you're not on my side, you're bad: a liar without courage. We live in an increasingly complex age, the roots of our past deeply buried, but not inaccessible. Doubt had encroached on me for too long, darkness had swallowed me whole—no longer. I leave no dark trail behind me. Follow the torches I have left behind. They mark the path.

Another fortnight passed with him away. I started to get jealous when he wouldn't respond to my messages, knowing he was with his mysterious boyfriend, but I'd put it out of my mind. I wasn't going to succumb to such weak emotions as jealousy.

The next time he came to visit, we dined out and

as usual Michael ordered for us. This time, none of it was for me. He knew I hadn't eaten all day and was hungry.

"I'll feed you later."

When we got back to the room he pulled out a bag of dog food and poured it into a bowl.

"Eat it," he said, pulling out his phone and filming me.

"You won't share that with anyone, right?"

"Anything I film is just for me, boy."

Then he held a knife to my chest, promising to carve it deep.

"Now, should I write an 'M' for Michael or a 'D' for a daddy?"

(An 'M', obviously.)

"I can't," I started crying.

He traced the letters the length of my pec, big enough to scare me. Without a shirt, there would be no hiding the scar. I stared into his eyes, tears streaming down my face, but not out of fear for the pain. A permanent mark seemed nice, given to me by someone that really wanted me, but he was living a double life while asking for my whole world. I broke down and begged him not to. He put his arms around me.

"Daddy will hold you while you bleed and cry."

I told him I couldn't do it. Not yet. He tried to push me through the fear of physical pain, but he didn't understand that wasn't the problem. He didn't understand I refused to be second best.

He was enraged when he threw some blankets in the corner, tied me up and gagged me down there, and went to bed.

"I wasn't going to do it," he said, spitefully, "you

failed the test."

I doubted the truth of that statement from this man that seemed to have no limits on my destruction, but that didn't stop me from feeling the worst about myself, as if I couldn't live up to his standard.

I lay there trying to push the gag out of my mouth, drooling over myself, asking if I really wanted to be nothing more than a beast. I slept. At some point I managed to untie myself and crawled into bed next to him. He didn't hold me that night.

I don't play games, he had said.

His birthday was coming up.

"What do you want?" I asked.

"Your blood," he said, and then, "Have you looked at the farm online?"

"No. Why would I do that?"

The suggestion seemed innocent. Of course, I wanted to know more about him, but I had been reluctant to look for any information about him, wary of any exposure to his partner and his life for fear of the jealousy it may provoke. But this invitation seemed to imply that it was safe to look. So, one day, feeling impermeable, I searched for him online and fell down a rabbit hole of style magazines, articles, photoshoots, interviews about how him and his partner met and how gloriously beautiful their lives were together. My confidence came crashing down as I saw them, arm in arm, with their hundreds of thousands of followers, their rich and famous friends. I hadn't had any idea.

Maybe he was right.

Maybe I was nothing more than a useless faggot.

I messaged him but his phone was off. His secret

phone. I didn't have his real number.

I passed the weekend in a pit of despair. It was Michael's birthday, and their anniversary. They posted a photo together on the beach.

I heard from him a few days later where, away from his boyfriend and family, he could safely access his other phone.

"This whole situation makes me feel sick. How can I commit to you like this when you have a boyfriend?"

"Stop being negative. Man up and take ownership."

"I'm trying to take ownership by asking for support."

"You couldn't handle me," he said, as if he treated his partner with the same brutality that he treated me with. Why did I not qualify for that kinder treatment, that extra sensitivity, after all the pain I was able to submit to?

"It is you that doesn't know how to handle me," I thought.

We argued and stopped talking.

And then the world stopped.

The borders closed. The pandemic hit.

I wouldn't see him for almost a year.

Just as soon as we could, we were back in each other's arms.

I was gagged and tied up and the biggest dildo was being crammed up inside me. I cried and tried to wriggle away but he had me pinned. A year earlier he hadn't even been able to get it inside—now he was trying to make me bleed on it, but I'd been practicing, expecting the worst. That didn't make it any more comfortable as he thrust it in and out of me and I screamed. He dragged me to the bathroom where he pissed down my throat.

"You spill a drop and I'll beat you so fucking hard, boy."

He took me back to the bed where he skullfucked me so relentlessly I puked my empty guts back up, nothing but his piss all over myself, and he still wouldn't stop fucking.

Upside down so his cock would go straight down my throat, I had a perfect view of the space between his balls and his asshole, and a single lump in between, a skin tag of some kind. It became a focal point while his balls were slapping against my nose and forehead, slap slap slap, and I would stare at this amidst my tears, trying to calm my breathing.

He whipped and beat me until I was bruised and blistered.

Then he'd ask me if I wanted the dildo or more whipping, enjoying my difficulty in picking the lesser torment, and knowing that he'd use both again anyway.

Eventually he came in me and we went to get some dinner.

"Why are you shaking?" he asked.

"Because you keep raping me."

He ordered me a double vodka, and himself a whiskey.

"I thought you weren't drinking," I said.

"Seeing you is a special occasion," he said. "You are marriage material. The day I give you a black eye… you'll know you're engaged."

My heart fluttered in my chest.

I waited on the curb, backpack slung across my back, the

small airport building blocking out the low sun. I shivered. I didn't bring much to keep me warm. I didn't think Orange would be this cold. Michael pulled around in his nice black truck, and I jumped in. We kissed.

"Happy birthday," I said, "I have a present for you."

Remembering what he had wanted from me a year earlier, I handed him my blood in a vial necklace. His eyes were glowing as he put it on.

"Did it hurt?"

He wanted me to say yes.

"No."

Nothing could have been easier. I felt no pain as long as it granted him pleasure, for it was the only thing that gave me purpose.

He pulled over on some dirt track and told me to get out of the car. I drank his piss by the side of the road before he fucked me on the bonnet. The sun was setting over the valley. Here it was warm. Everything was gold except the red of my blood dancing amongst the fur of his chest. I looked at my wrist, no bracelet, and wondered if he would ever give me that gift—if I was still that same boy to him that I was on the beach.

"I'm going to send you home a different boy," he told me.

Back in the car, he whipped out a bottle of premium whiskey and told me to drink. I kept spluttering as I tried to drink it straight and he kept forcing more down my throat. I was dizzy by the time we pulled into the estate. Beyond the great gates the long gravel driveway was lined with trees, ostriches running up and down the fields, horses and pigs in the distance, a lake with a small rowing boat, the beautiful farmhouse. I stepped out into the garden, into paradise.

He kept forcing the whiskey down my throat as he stripped me down, pulled out a hard leather rod, and a thinner, leather whip. He started with the rod until I was covered in bruises. Then he dragged me into another building, the servant quarters. Strange wooden beams were connected to the ceiling, meant for hanging dead animals maybe, and he strung me up to them. He set up a camera and filmed, beating me until I cried.

He shaved my head and I stared down the lens of the camera, stared at my unknown audience, as if to ask them: who is really in control here?

"Beautiful," he said, kissing me.

He tied me over a log and came in me, my mouth taped shut, leaving me there as he packed away his torture devices. The dog came over to sniff me, then started licking my ass. I couldn't move.

"That pussy tastes good, doesn't it?" he asked when he walked back in.

He dragged me back into the kitchen and made me drink more, snapping the key off in a chastity cage, locking it permanently before making us dinner. I sat at the dining table, my head spinning, barely able to see, unable to eat a thing.

"Bed time, boy. Upstairs."

I went where I was directed, the bedroom on the first landing, *the blue room*, he called it. I swayed, drunk, gazing out the window at the lake and the animals. He came in behind me, turned me around, kept me from falling over, and we kissed while he lit a match. He held me firmly as he put it out on my stomach. I didn't feel a thing as he put out two more on my belly.

"I love you, boy," he said.

"I love you too."

We kissed harder as he put the last one out on my ass.

I heard muffled noises downstairs. My head hurt and next to me the bed was empty. The grey morning had barely started and I could just trace the outline of the rocky hills out the window. I did not want to be without him and pulled the blankets off me to find they had stuck to my seeping wounds during the night, my ass to the sheets beneath me and my belly to the covers. Downstairs he sat at the table, staring into the distance.

"Are you going for your walk?

"Yes."

"Can I come?"

"Sure."

We jumped in the car and drove into town. He bought us coffees and we walked a long route through the park where I swallowed his strong morning piss. As we walked, I was unable to find the words for my overflowing emotion, and all the affection I desired from him.

"I could get arrested for what I've done to you," he said.

"I'd never report you to the police."

All I wanted was to be with him, but it felt stilted, like in that moment the reality of me was encroaching over the divide between his life and his fantasy, worlds he wanted to keep separate. But I wasn't just a fantasy. I was living, and breathing, and walking the streets of Orange—a real human being. Not just a faggot.

Back at the estate, I was told to spend the day naked in bed so I wouldn't be seen by the staff. I mostly did what I was told, staring out the window at the countryside, the hills and chickens out one side, the lake and ostriches out the other. I was happy, I think. A few times I wandered into his office, showing off my bruises and the wounds.

"Do you think these will scar?" I asked, concerned about the deep holes made from the matches.

"Pfft," he laughed, "no, you'll know when I do that to you."

Eventually the staff left. I went to ask if he needed any help.

"Sure. You can go up to the back paddock and make sure the horses have water."

So off I went, passed the long outdoor table and fireplace, the vegetable gardens, the chickens and the pit being dug for the pool, behind the old barn and through the gate. The horses came up to greet me, two great beautiful beasts. The trough was still full of water, so I gave them a pat and decided to explore the gardens.

I wandered towards the lake, passing a strange but grand pillar with an empty plaque, a monument to his dead dog. This I took as evidence that he could feel love, though I thought of Ozymandias and wondered to what portion it was just his own ego. The ostriches seemed excited by me, but I kept a distance, their great necks and strong legs capable of tearing me to pieces. Then, as I wandered up to the house, by the front stairs I passed a bench with another plaque, something I had missed arriving drunk and in darkness the evening before.

13th MARCH 2021
FOR MICHAEL WHO LOVES THIS GARDEN
FROM STEVE WHO ALWAYS SITS BESIDE HIM
HAPPY BIRTHDAY

Again, that feeling of being punched in the stomach. I checked my phone. Today was the 17th. I could not flee even if I wanted to—where would I go? I was in the middle of the country. I imagined the weekend, four days earlier, another birthday, another of their anniversaries, Michael being led out the front terrace and unveiled this gift of undying love, their families watching on lovingly. All the peace and tranquillity I had fostered vanished as I plummeted again into the depths of despair. I was an invader in this space. I had believed their love was dead, that I was the new growth, but this sick feeling told me I was just a weed.

I walked into his office where he was working.

"Did you have a nice walk?"

"The horses have plenty of water. I saw the ostriches… and… the bench out the front."

He didn't look up from his laptop. He just kept tapping on his keyboard. The silence lasted a lifetime. Eventually he stood up.

"Well, I'm going into town. I've got to get a few things. Do you want to come?"

"Sure."

I sat quietly in the car down the long driveway.

"Are you ok?" he asked, eventually, as we pulled onto the road.

"I don't know… I just—"

He pulled off into a driveway directly across the

road.

"Ok, the quarry's up here. Do you want to come up for a walk?" he interrupted.

A gated road led up an overgrown hill.

"Sure."

We jumped the fence and waded through huge weeds, passed some confused looking cows, up to a giant manmade hole full of water. He fiddled with a pump, got the water flowing back across the road to the farm, a long hose stretching through a drainpipe down the hill. I waited, thinking he'd ask again about this emotional tension that hung so heavily in the air, a tension he had dismembered into the background just as quickly as he'd acknowledged it. But he didn't. We jumped back in the car and drove into town where he picked up some timber, spoke to a lady on the phone about buying chickens, and I sat in the passenger seat trying to wrestle my anxiety into submission, to not be bothered by this glamorous, successful, beautiful, loving relationship that stood in the way of what I wanted.

We stopped at a café.

"Do you want anything? Coffee? A juice?"

"No thanks. I'll have something stronger when we get home."

"Do you think you have a drinking problem?" he asked.

(You're my fucking drinking problem.)

"Maybe."

How could I express to him that in front of me was the life I had always dreamed of, supporting a successful man in his projects, getting fucked by him non-stop, giving him everything in one of the most beautiful places I had ever been—only to be denied the reality of it all, and at the end of the day, sent home, nobody knowing I was ever there, for his partner to come and settle into bed with him, the sheets washed, my weeping wounds leaving nothing more than a small stain. "I love you," they would whisper to each other, and I would be all alone, an unsaved number and a to-be deleted conversation on a second, secret phone, hidden in the glove compartment of his truck.

Of course I wanted a fucking drink.

"Ok, make yourself a drink," he said when we arrived back.

I poured a gin and tonic, waiting anxiously for some emotional support as he pottered about the kitchen, made a sandwich, responded to an email. When he was done, he started to head upstairs.

"I thought we were going to talk," I cried.

He stood at the bottom of the stairs and looked at me pitifully.

"I don't think there's anything to discuss."

"Please," I begged.

"Fine."

He took me to the lounge.

"I think you're looking for things to be upset about," he said, "I want you to have fun."

I didn't know how to explain to him that I loved this. That I felt powerful and exhilarated with him, that he provided me with a way to demonstrate just how much I could take, how much pain I could withstand to give a man pleasure—but that it all seemed to mean nothing if I had to run away and hide when his boyfriend came home, that I'd never meet his friends, that I was supposed to let him pierce and scar my body while I waited around for him to maybe put me first. That I was supposed to give him my whole life while he treated me like an option.

"I came down here to have fun and enjoy my time with you. It's not like I was walking around looking for benches engraved four days ago. But if I don't talk about this and express it, it's just going to keep making me feel sick and I won't be able to have fun with you and be that boy you want me to be. You said it's important we are totally honest with each other and I agree. So, I need to tell you how I feel. I need to get this out of my system."

Michael told me that the bench was nothing more than a ploy for their followers to worship them, that it would be rotting and falling apart in a year with no one to care for it, that anyone who knew him knew that if he was in the garden he was working, not sitting down. He also told me he didn't have time for my emotional problems: that his boyfriend had anxiety and depression, was struggling against his own monsters, and that he had to spend all of his time helping him.

"I can't help you with your mental illness too," he said, "maybe you should see a therapist."

I felt slightly better knowing the man who was my opposition was struggling in the depths of my conquered territory.

"I don't have any mental illness. Not anymore. But introduce me to Steve," I said, "I can help him."

He laughed at me.

"No you can't. We pay $700 a session for someone to do that."

"I have spent my entire life doing this," I said, thinking surely this successful man who has fought for me so passionately would witness me, not believing he could be part of the uninitiated.

"You don't know anything about this stuff. Psychiatrists study for years to learn it all."

"I do, and I'm an artist," I said, "I think he would like me."

"He wouldn't like you," Michael shook his head, "and you're not an artist. An artist is a painter."

Did he really believe I was nothing more than a useless faggot to be destroyed? Could he really not see all it was I gave him, and all that I yet had to offer?

"I just don't understand how you can have all this, this beautiful house, this beautiful life, your partner who loves you and makes all this money—how could you ever walk away from this?"

"I'm a simple man. I don't need much to be happy," he said, and I didn't know how to point out the irony of him making that statement when he had more than anyone I knew.

"I would much rather be in a relationship with you. But let's not get carried away. We just need to take this one step at a time. I don't want to lead you down the garden path."

A thoughtful sentiment considering we were having this conversation in said garden. But there was no reason trying to argue.

"Ok," I said, always locked into a silence, knowing that the truth would tear us apart. He did not want me for the truth. He wanted me only for my body, and with every moment it broke my heart.

"Make another drink. Watch a movie. I've got work to do."

I looked down at the wounds on my stomach, still weeping. Would they scar?

Pfft, no.

I put them out of my mind.

Let's not get carried away.

He wanted me to trust him.

You're just looking for things to be upset about.

My eyes traced the sculptures and the paintings, and the ugly candles on the mantlepiece, and I wondered if this perfect life would ever be mine.

A delivery truck arrived. Michael came downstairs and unloaded some timber and tarps. Daylight was running out so I helped, spent an hour or two mowing the lawns, and then rain was coming so we had to cover the pit for the pool. I was down in the hole when the groundskeeper John appeared out of nowhere to assist us. I glanced at Michael to check his reaction. Nothing changed on his face.

"Is this one of Peter's boys?" John asked. I was almost thirty but this man thought I was sixteen.

"No, those boys are gladiators," Michael said, and I was emasculated by the discussion of these apparently hulking teenage boys half my age, even though I was the one down in the hole doing the heavy lifting—but the arena of my battles never had an audience.

"I'm a gladiator," I said, though Michael, as usual, did not heed me.

"We're all gladiators in our own way," said John.

The questioning over my identity went no further. We covered the pit and the groundskeeper left. We went back inside.

"Take two of these," Michael said, holding out some Valium. I was anxious and looked at them, tempted, but was vaguely aware that I might have to defend myself tonight. He dragged me back to the servant quarters, roping me up once again.

The previous night I had been resilient to the punishment. Tonight, already bruised and beaten, my cold body was so sore and sensitive that the same punishments hurt much worse. He blindfolded and gagged me, and I heard the familiar sound of a match being lit. I was already crying.

"No," I muffled.

Through the blindfold I could see the barest glimmer of light, an indication of what direction the match was coming from. I no longer trusted his verdict on the scarring and waited until the last millisecond, the match right on my skin before surprising him and thrashing my body around, preventing him from pushing them in like he did the night before. He lit match after match in this way and I could hear his frustration as I avoided the burns, my frantic struggling preventing any from breaking the top layer of my skin. At least in that moment I knew what was best for me. What if I had taken the Valium? My body would have been ruined.

Eventually he fucked me, blew in my ass and we went back inside to watch a movie.

"So, can I ask you a question?" he said.

It was our last night together before I flew back to Brisbane. Ask me anything, I thought.

"Of course."

"What do you really think of the farm?"

Oh.

"You've created something beautiful. I'm blown away."

"Thanks, boy. Is there anything you think could

be better?"

I looked up at the mantelpiece, at the ugly candles I'd noticed that afternoon.

"I hate those candles."

"Those were $700 each."

And like your boyfriend's psychiatrist sessions, probably about as good.

But I felt again as if I had been punched in the stomach. I did some quick math. There was about $10,000 just on the shelf. More money than I'd seen in my life.

"Well, whose decision was that?" I asked.

"Good question," he scowled.

The next day he went on his walk. I didn't go with him. When he came back, I helped him mow the front yard by the gate, and a neighbour stopped to talk to us. He lived across the road and told me about the Chinese miners who settled on the land a hundred years earlier, how the mine collapsed, and how they had to seal it off because all the bodies were still down there. We said goodbye, and riding the quad bike around the property, feeling the wind against my shaved head, I was glad not to be dead at the bottom of a hole yet. I fed the ostriches and made myself useful. I wanted to stay forever.

But we were out of time.

He was meant to take me to the airport.

"Shit. I'm sorry, boy. I don't have time. I'm going to have to call you a cab."

I pretended not to be upset.

Half an hour later, we kissed goodbye. I was headed down the long drive and the driver kept asking me about the estate, question after question, and I was forced to explain Michael and his partner, the income from his corporate job he barely attended that fed this luxurious lifestyle, everything I did not have. I winced when I had to pay $70 for the cab ride. I could feel my shirt sticking to my stomach, and my jeans to my ass.

I returned home in a fog. I did not know how to fly at these great heights. A little higher and the sun might have melted the wax. I was choking in the stale mist.

At home, I lay in the sun, confused and disoriented. I stared at the black bruises all over my body, the deep match wounds that had now turned a milky white, like holes dug into my skin then filled with a strange cream.

I didn't know what to do. I had dinner with my friends, and asked for advice.

"He's not going to leave his boyfriend," one said, "if he wanted to be with you, he would be."

"You don't know that. He might."

"Bullshit, he's just using you."

"He's not!" I said, exasperated, "I love him!"

"Finally, you said it!"

He rolled his eyes. We laughed.

"I do. I love him. And he said he loves me."

I barely slept that night, trying to make sense of this strange feeling creeping over me. I messaged Michael but heard nothing back.

Another friend, a nurse, looked at my wounds.

"Jesus Christ. I'm really worried about you."

"I'm fine."

"You're clearly not fine. This man is going to run through you like a train."

"I can take it. That's how I get stronger."

"You'll learn to love the pain", Michael had told

me, "Pain feels good, doesn't it?"

Why did it feel like he was the only one being honest with me about what I was expected to put myself through?

"He's going to destroy you."

The wounds were starting to get infected and the nurse took me to the pharmacist where we got special silver bandages and disinfectant, returning home to apply them.

"If these get infected, or if you start to get a fever, you need to go to the hospital straight away," he told me.

Then I couldn't control my breathing. I was on the floor sobbing, grabbing the cock cage still attached to my body and managing to rip it in two with my hands. The hospital? Michael had told me it wouldn't even scar. I wanted to call the police, to scream, to cry out, but if I did that I would never have him, never prove myself strong enough. Why was it that no matter what course of action I chose, I always lost?

"They're definitely going to scar, James."

"Ok," I cried.

Over the next two weeks I spent hundreds of dollars on special silver bandages. The silver would draw the moisture out and help them heal faster. But he had marked me, just how he wanted.

That afternoon I spoke to him on the phone.

"I freaked out and broke the cage off," I told him.

"Why did you do that?"

"I don't know. It's just... I'm in love with you. I know you said you don't want to rush things, but I've known you for almost two years now. I know how I feel. I love you."

"I love you too, boy."

"It's just so painful. My nurse friend told me these burns will scar. I just can't have this relationship with you and let you do these permanent things to me while you're with someone else."

"Well, it sounds like you've made up your mind," he said, "if you think you can find something better, you're welcome to go find it."

My heart shattered.

"No," I cried.

That night I dreamt I was back at the farm. I was in the kitchen with the two of them. I was kissing Steve deeply. Michael brought in ropes and tied me up while he watched in surprise, shocked as his partner belted me and I cried. Then, they shared me. As I sucked Steve's cock, staring up at him, his eyes were full of love.

I woke up and everything felt alright.

"I thought about what you said yesterday," Michael messaged me, "and I'm still going to do whatever I want to you."

"Like I said, just nothing permanent. It upsets me too much."

"I think you're just used to getting what you want, boy," he said.

No, I'm used to having to fight for every scrap, is what I wanted to say. *I'm used to people ignoring me, preferring their delusions about reality over my insights. I'm used to being put down and told I'm nothing to the point that it's become a life skill. You, on the other hand – a private school prefect that didn't bother questioning his sexuality until the age of twenty-seven – you are used to getting what you want. It's just that you're living a lie while I'm living the truth, and from your perspective, that looks like I have what I want, because actually I have what you want; a freedom born of truth alone. What I want is a little bit of power, to protect myself, and to have earned the respect of my people, something you seem to have innately. If you were to tell me that I cannot take anything with me from this life, well, I would agree with you, as that is exactly how I have lived: maximising beauty, pleasure, and truth for all. But that is not how you have lived. You have put yourself before truth and therefore betrayed not just me, but all that are like us. You say you are a simple man. I think you are decidedly so, for you know the truth but choose to ignore it while it begets you power.*

Of course, I did not say these things. I was terrified of being disposable to him, especially after I had given so much of myself over. I couldn't focus on anything but him. Everything in my life felt pointless. A month earlier, I was content with everything, but now, none of it had any value. If I wasn't with Michael, I couldn't see the point. I knew how unhealthy that was, how ridiculous that was, but I couldn't seem to fix my own perspective. I was fighting to reclaim control over my own value, doing whatever I could to get his tendrils out. Understanding his psychology – the truth of how and why he valued me – was a balm on that pain.

I never fail at anything, he had said, a year earlier.

But what was his criteria for failure or success? At the time, I understood him to mean that he would take care of me, that I would be safe under his power, if only I handed mine over. Now, looking back, it seems more likely that his intention was purely to cause me more pain than anyone else while getting his rocks off, and failure in this case was not marked by his inability to provide emotional support but instead by impotency. By his definition, as long as my asshole was bred and I was covered in more bruises than anyone else had ever given me, he had succeeded. He wasn't interested in my criteria. I became something to be destroyed, and any emotional repercussions of our time together was categorised by him as my own weakness, not a shortcoming of his, and certainly not a failure. Any problems I had were psychological issues of my own to be sorted out by a psychiatrist—certainly not something he or anyone else had caused me.

I went to Sporties, tried to drink and socialise, tried to make my life feel meaningful without him. I told another friend, Max, about the situation.

"Why are you still seeing this dickhead?" he asked.

"I don't know. I've already got the scars. Sunk cost fallacy?" I joked.

"That's why I like you," he laughed, "you're smarter than these men give you credit for. Smarter than this dumb twink façade."

"Yeah but no one likes a smart twink, apparently."

I kept changing the bandages on my wounds, and slowly they healed into a bright pink, but in the heat of the shower they would go a deep, dark molten red. I went up the coast to get away, a holiday, trying to get away from my own negative thoughts. I met a man and showed him my scars. One day he knocked on the door of my room and as soon as I opened it he had his hands around my throat, kissing me and pushing me onto the bed, but his hands only simulating choking, not really applying any pressure, and I told him to leave, apologising; I was in love with someone else, and I craved only Michael's firm and brutal grip.

Finally, Michael messaged me to tell me he needed me. He flew me from the coast the next day.

"I'm going to get your cock pierced tomorrow."

"Let's save that for the day I'm your boyfriend."

"It's a pity all your marks have healed."

Did he even pay attention?

"They haven't. You've permanently scarred me."

"I'll bring more matches tomorrow."

"No," I cried, "I never want to say no to you. But I can't. Why don't you understand?"

And he went quiet.

I went to sleep with that familiar sick feeling back in my stomach. All I wanted was his approval, his love, but he didn't care about my feelings, didn't want to know. All this meant was that I wasn't strong enough for him.

He didn't respond to my messages until midday the next day, just as I was boarding my flight to Sydney.

"Boarding soon. Haven't heard from you. Did I say something wrong?"

"You pissed me off last night. When you try to say no it's a massive turnoff. I'll feel better after I make you cry."

"I feel like I have Stockholm Syndrome."

"What's that?" he asked.

He picked me up from the airport and drove us straight to the hotel, making me suck his cock or skull whiskey from the bottle the entire drive.

"You're not wearing the necklace," I said.

"Sorry, boy, I knew you'd notice. I love it. I've been wearing it all the time, I promise."

"Really? Has Steve seen you wearing it?"

"Yep."

"Did he say anything?"

"Yeah, he just said, *you got a necklace.*"

"What did you say?"

"I said, *yep.*"

I couldn't believe I was right on display, that Steve had seen my blood. My sense of value came back, like a fucked-up tide that kept leaving me emotionally stranded, returning and abandoning me again.

We arrived at the hotel and he started beating me again, forcing more whiskey down my throat, and shoving fruit and vegetables up my ass, all big and colourful ones that someone might have liked to put in a bowl and paint. I could not say no. I needed him.

My body heaved as I sat crumpled underneath the hot shower, waiting outside myself for the adrenaline to pass. When we went to dinner, I was so drunk and my ass so full of banana that I had to go to the bathroom and take turns throwing up and pushing fruit fragments out of my hole. I returned to the table, the room spinning. Michael was staring at another table.

"I can't stop looking at that fat bitch on her date. I mean, it's good they have each other, but I don't get it."

"People connect over more than just physical attraction," I said.

He shrugged. Was this his way of complimenting me? My beauty had brought me close to him.

I started to copy his movements, learned from him, for indeed he had been worshipped for his cruelty. While I had been seen as having nothing to offer, incapable of responsibility, he had been chosen like the others as a captain. He thought I had nothing to offer him except my flesh, and so I was as invisible to him as I had been to all before him. I was nothing but a loyal dog, though I was a mutt only while kept in poverty. He did not see how I rattled the bars—and if he recognised my cage he did not acknowledge it. He would deliver my freedom one way or another, I would make sure of that, though for the moment, I had to betray myself.

Another two weeks passed before he flew me down again, taking me straight from the airport to some beach called Little Congwong. The sun was low in the empty blue sky. Everything was tranquil as we walked around the headland. I was sad to be somewhere so beautiful again, knowing it made every moment with him more painful.

"How old are you? Forty-six?"

"Yep."

"My favourite age," I smiled at him.

"My favourite age is sixteen," he said, "I think I should turn you in for a younger boy."

My youth diminishes, I thought, as does yours. If this is how you show someone you love them, no wonder your boyfriend is trapped in the abyss.

His words echoed back to me.

You couldn't handle me, he had said.

"A younger boy couldn't handle you," I said.

We went down to the rocks where he fucked me in front of a crowd, choking me until I passed out over a branch, coming back to consciousness seconds later, the world a strange hue of blue, reminding me of those years a long time ago, passing out in the Manual Arts shed, the stars crossing my vision.

On the drive to the hotel, he opened up.

"I want you to have fun. But if this isn't fun for you, we need to stop."

"I can deal with the physical pain. The problem is as long as you are in a relationship, this is going to cause me emotional pain. I can't be a secret."

"Maybe you need to see a therapist to talk about your anxiety problems," he repeated.

"I don't have anxiety problems. You're the only thing in my life that causes me emotional distress."

"Really?"

"Yeah, apart from this, I'm fine. Or I was fine. But now it's like everything in my life is losing value. I can't focus on anything. I can't get you out of my head. I'm terrified you're using me, that I don't really exist in your life. I just feel disposable and awful about myself and that's not going to change until you leave Steve, or tell him about me."

"I think we need to stop. I don't want to hurt you."

"Maybe."

At the hotel room, I used his phone to send myself the videos he had made of me, the ones of him shaving my head at the barn. I glanced through his messages, wanting the same insight into his life that he had into mine.

A text from an unsaved number read "hey princess". Princess? He hadn't replied.

"Do you ever bottom?" I asked.

"Nope," he shrugged. I couldn't tell what was him and what was the version he wanted me to see.

He had a few messages back and forth with a contact called Double Trouble – I suspected a couple he had threesomes with.

An unsaved number said, "can you come into the café again?"—a barista he'd fucked?

And then, one number with a lot of chatting, including a video of me. My jealousy and anger spiked.

"I thought you weren't going to share these videos with anyone," I stared at him, showing him the phone screen.

"He's not even in the country. Why does it matter?"

"It has my face in it. I don't know who this person is. You lied. You told me you wouldn't share these."

His eyes opened wide, just for a second, as he realised the kind of trouble he might be in.

"I'm sorry, boy. I won't do it again."

I forgave him. At least, I tried to, as he held me down and fucked me, and I stared into his eyes, tears welling in my own, my body full of rage.

"I can't do this to you," he said.

Then he came.

We slept together in one of the two single beds the hotel had given us that night, a tight fit, cuddling, aware it was our last night together.

"I feel good. I feel like we're making the right decision," I said the next morning.

He got on top of me, breeding me again.

"I'm going to miss this pussy," he said.

We showered and brushed our teeth.

"We'll see each other again in the future," he said, the toothbrush still in my mouth.

My eyes filled with tears again.

"Don't cry," he said, "we're making the right decision."

Then he was rushing out the door. He couldn't even get his car out of the carpark for another twenty minutes.

"Wait, you're going?"

"Bye, boy."

The door shut behind him. Like that, he was gone.

I glanced around the room. A Stanley knife lay by the television, and one of his T-shirts was crumpled under the chair. I picked it up, held it to my nose, thought about putting it in my bag. I threw it back on the floor. I took just my own things and walked to the station, caught the train to the airport. I felt strong, like nothing could touch me, but tears were streaming down my face the entire way. I couldn't stop them as I watched the Opera House and the Harbour Bridge pass by. I held composure, not sobbing, not moving, but the flood of tears continued as I got off the train, waited in the airport, took the plane, the car ride home, my body stoic and unmoving but the drops saturating my mask and falling relentlessly off my chin. As soon as I walked into my bedroom I collapsed, sobbing and heaving on the floor.

I did everything I could to reclaim my sense of self. Every night I was out drinking at bars and nightclubs, but I could not escape him.

I had breakfast with a new friend, but Michael was right there on the coffee table, front and centre of a magazine, him and his partner in loving embrace.

"That's him," I cried.

"I bought it because I thought the dog was cute," he said, trying to make me feel better.

"That dog has licked my asshole," I said, staring through the floor.

He looked at me in shock.

"That's disgusting."

I remembered the pain of Dylan thanking Jeremy on stage for all he had done. This was a hundredfold. I looked from the cigarette burn on my arm to the fresh scars on my stomach and I wondered how I might carry the burden of this flame, rise like a phoenix from the ashes, Antinous from the depths, a vanguard in the darkness with nothing but anger as fuel to relight the long-forgotten torches of my divided tribe.

I danced all night and took pills with big beary men who kissed me and fingered me and passed me around. I posted a photo of myself in a mesh top surrounded by a gang of them, and that was all he could take. Michael blocked me.

On one hand I was elated – I could still evoke a jealousy in him that forced him to react, which meant he wanted me. On the other hand, I was pissed off. I had trudged through so much bullshit and jealousy for him, and yet, he could not cope with a single photo of me nightclubbing? I wanted to scream at him: "Where is your resilience? Where is your empathy for what I've been through?"

Still, I could not stop thinking of him. I remembered how he had rushed out of the hotel room the last time we had seen each other when he had told me not to cry. At the time I thought he had been callous to leave so quickly. Now I wondered if he had been scared of crying in front of me. I had visions of tears flowing down his face as he drove back to his farm that day. I wondered if he missed me as much as I missed him.

I doubted it.

A few weeks later he unblocked me. He sent me a message. I resisted responding with all my might. He would block me again, though this would be the last time I would hear from him.

"I can't stop thinking and wanking about you."

∴

"If you ever cared for him, he needs you now more than ever."

Andy sent me this message explaining the dire situation Jacob was in—all this from the man that had caused the destruction. Why was I expected to pick up the pieces? Was I a god? I despised his insinuation of my guilty absence as if my life should similarly orbit the object of his desires—that which he simultaneously and actively destroyed. If it fell to me to hold the world together though, I believed I could, if only I was given the power to do it.

I did not respond to Andy, but I called Jacob.

He told me he had moved in with him. He had run out of options and wanted to make a go of the relationship, but Andy would leave for work and Jacob would spend the day in Andy's garden, doing his best to make it beautiful. Andy would get home and Jacob would show him his work, though Andy was always unimpressed by his efforts; Jacob cried telling me this. Then they would fight. He wasn't being provided with the good cocaine anymore, just crystal meth. Now that his bird was caged, he no longer loved it. Its beauty had been in its wildness.

It was Christmas but Andy wouldn't let him leave. Jacob drove his car, smashing into the garage door again and again until Andy finally released him.

No one seems to know where he spent that Christmas. He never made it to see his family.

On Boxing Day, he returned to Andy's place.

And the next morning, they each woke up, alone.

Andy found Jacob's car by the cliffs.

Then they found Jacob, twisted and broken on the rocks below.

I cried to my friends.

"You can never understand why someone makes that decision," one of them said.

But I knew exactly why, and I had all this rage, none of which I knew what to do with.

Two-thousand years ago, Antinous drowned, and Hadrian declared his death a mystery. I find that almost impossible to believe. It seems that nothing has changed in all this time and that our stories are ignored on purpose. I want to believe that a man like Hadrian could exist. I want to believe I could be good enough for him. I want to believe I could be him. Were Antinous and Jacob not murdered? A king merely calls it sacrifice because our young blood nourishes their soul—but it is murder. Our narratives are erased, time and again—powerless against the men that use and destroy us. Somehow, I walked to the end of that path and found myself, not dead as intended, but with a rebirth. I had attempted to sacrifice myself for a great man, but I am not sure a Hadrian exists in our time, or if he ever did. Instead I am left with this feeling, unsure if it is love or hate, either way a sick obsession, but an obsession for which I do not feel guilty, for if he didn't want me to be this way then why did he brand me? Well, I need to live the rest of my life, and like the frozen legs of the Swedish military, I have subjected myself, my emotions, to my own life training. My heart is numbed and now I seek to warm it in a friendly armpit. I cannot continue any further without some acknowledgment of what has occurred and all I am capable of. I am covered in bruises and scars. I know how to play rough. My strength has been displayed. I am one of the boys. I will be denied no longer. I have fought in the meaningless trenches of the abyss long enough. Send someone else down there that needs to learn. It is not me.

Antinous sacrificed himself no more than Jacob did. Loved only for their beauty and innocence, they were forced into death when they could no longer serve their singularly allowed purpose. I will not suffer the same end as those boys who could not stand up to their tormentors.

It is time my presence is known. I seek to love a great man. I am no naïve youth. Hadrian worshipped Antinous for being a youth without aspiration, though that was a lie and a façade—it is a simple feat to hide one's motivations, especially from powerful men who wish to see nothing but blind youth and, indeed, specifically train us to hide such motives, punishing us for wanting anything. It was not Antinous blind to aspiration but Hadrian blind to his own lust. Now I have turned the tables. I don't care anymore. Take it all, all I have—books upon books. I need them less.

Andy sat in the backrow at the funeral, gigantic sunglasses to hide his eyes red from tears, not for Jacob whom he claimed to love, but for himself—he cried for he could not admit his own cruel nature. He got exactly what he wanted.

Andy, the stage master, the victim.

You caged your bird, not just clipping its wings but severing them from its body, and cried when it died. What did you expect? I cannot repair your pet this time, fractured beyond even the power of my vines.

I will die before you control me.

∴

It had been a year.

I had a dream. You were cradling me and lay me down in a bath. You kissed me gently, looked into my eyes and said, "I'm going to tell Steve about you". I was overcome with pleasure. You saw the tears well up in my eyes before going to find him. I awaited your return, walking through the gardens when I heard a man screaming, hideous and bone-chilling. I ran to the house and saw a stranger lying on the driveway, legs broken and twisted. He saw me and howled louder, coming closer, slowly, crawling. I locked myself in the house. Your house. I tried to hide but I could not escape his wailing, and then his banging on the windowpanes. He was desperate for my assistance. Who was this man? Did you do this to him? Do I call an ambulance or wait for you to return, to finish him off? Where are you?

I woke up in a sweat.

I had another dream. I found you behind your desk. Steve is there and asks who I am. In that moment he discovers your secret life and now it is him screaming, wailing, attacking you.

Again, I woke up in a sweat.

This happened while I was on a road-trip with Josh as he escaped from his abusive ex-partner, down the east coast to his terrace house, and he saw the turn in my mood.

"I didn't drive one-thousand kilometers to get away from a sadistic fuckwit for you to be depressed over another sadistic fuckwit."

And then I was laughing, and the tears were rolling down my face. I went to Bondi Beach; my first time there. The two of you must have been nearby. I dug my toes into the sand.

What are you trying to do? Make me lose my shit? Well consider my shit lost.

I have fucked all your husbands and as the object of their desires I am the reality that none can face. No longer. Taste the honey and descend into madness, for what is murder? What is assault? What is a victim? Take me to the court—I have armed and trained myself, and although I may be delicate and soft, my heart is strong, and I will fight until death, but cowards, the lot of you. You dare not come for me except in the shadows and behind closed doors.

Was it an ulterior motive that I didn't really want to be destroyed? I wanted him to love me.

I want you to have fun.

I'll tell him what would be fun: to tell the truth and finally have it heard. For my life to no longer be conducted in secret for the sake of men with power who cannot admit their shame. Will he be happy for me now that I have done this?

What of him now?

I do not think he will come to me. He may come for me, and if he does, what else will he be permitted to take? And what of his debt? He who was the greatest and most wretched thing to occur to me, with the blood and the scars that tie us still. He is not one to acknowledge another's power, certainly not mine… and yet, maybe he will come.

My great love, little man, how to blow you from

the water, how to forget you completely?

With this act do I sever our ties or strengthen them, and if it's both, what does that mean? Is everything it's opposite? Let's see which way this goes. I am freed of reckoning by the scars themselves, those very marks which imprison me, and not for the last time I exist in polarity; love and hate, anxiety and excitement, good and evil, freedom and slavery, the great and the wretched. Through their sameness I am given life.

These pathetic men… Jacob, if only you had the mind to handle such a strength as yours. Now I know it was not my blood I was seeking but yours: oil for the lamps that show the way. I return the truth and pleasure to myself and the people. Let no man own me but give me the restitutions to be independent. Am I not owed this by a nation to which I have given all? Not in the way that was asked of me, I understand, for I do not think you knew what it was you were asking for. I have given you what you really wanted.

There, now, it is done, do you see?

With my thyrsus I light the torches,

and the flame dances after me.

My swollen and burned heart yet beats fiercely.

"Tell Steve about me, give me some money, anything that validates my place in your life," I had asked—but he smirked and laughed when he said, "no, but it sounds like you've made up your mind," and I could see the sadistic glint in his eye, the emotional pain he knew he had caused me, the same look George gave me twenty years earlier when he knocked me down in class, the same question hidden behind those eyes: *what are you going to do about it?* It's clear he didn't want to let me in, that he never wanted to let me in. He wanted to evoke desire within me and to destroy me with his power.

I collapsed into nothingness.

All the pain from my years of abjection and all the love I felt for my fellow man came together in this one figurehead. He could have let me in, he could have stood up against the tide, he who claims to fail at nothing, but he proved to be without courage, to let me be washed away in a flood of tears.

But I did not move. Not this time.

I do not need anyone to grant me my position in this world. I shall take it for myself.

I bring this arena to light.

My body bears the marks of the silent war I am in. Is my war not the core of all others? I know I am not blinded by ego, for I see it in all other things. Discard me, nothing more than a secret number on the burner phone, discard me at the peril of all, for if love is not the point, then what else?

I'm tired of this secret battle. Let this attempt shine on your iron fist, if only for a moment, and may all see the truth.

This was Hadrian all along, throwing Antinous overboard.

But the matches held to my flesh were not enough to melt the wax from my wings, and I soar in with the corpse of innocence at my feet.

What power is this? My thyrsus is ripe.

I am out for blood and reap my harvest with great delight.

Just like out of thin air, baby—*poof!* I was here all along.

Now who is going to show me a good time, or am I the only one that knows how to throw a god-damned party?

Men, behind me. I take ground.

Saint Genet, Veronica Franco, I hold you in my heart.

I am at breaking point.

I have let things go, time and again, but no longer. Now I'm not letting *anything* go.

Don't worry, it's not like any of you are on your own. It's been a community effort, has it not? Maybe you can have a class action against me too. Well, this is my attempt at the solicitation of justice in the modern age. Or didn't you know that's how the real world works? The power of law-and-order ebbs against chaos.

In truth, I will submit to any man or woman that is truly more powerful, more deserving of power than I, and they will have my utmost respect and loyalty. But to the men and women that I have so far been forced to concede I see nothing but weakness.

Am I alone in witnessing this? It cannot be.

The silence is deafening.

I am powerless, adrift in chaos.

And now, how to claw back this power? I put pen to paper.

I have been collecting pain for a long time, pain that does not belong to me, shouldering a burden that is not mine alone to carry. I hand all this pain back, ornately dressed—a gift. This pain needs to be released somehow, as every action needs its reaction, and this is the only way I can see of releasing it and minimising destruction, like a nuclear detonation in an isolated ocean. A few fish are necessary casualties, as the very practice of defence is necessary; for my own protection, and, though it may not look like it at first, that of this nation and this world. If I am found guilty of telling the truth, of defamation, well, so be it. That says more about the state of things than about my state of being. I know what I have to offer, what I have offered, and how it has gone unnoticed, unappreciated, despite our collectively professed virtues. I also know what happens when I attempt to defend myself: I am further punished. A country of criminals this is—maybe a criminal penalty is exactly what I need to finally belong to our kind. Let me face up to my fate, whatever it may be. I know I have enough evidence to make a case for myself. The question is whether those who witness what comes next can stare into the abyss as I have done—that will be the true test of my fate. Out of my hands, then, and into that of the jury. How blessed I am to live on this precipice where the status quo has not already won by default, and what an exciting future: to be guilty or innocent, I agree to be satisfied by anything except being complicit in my own silencing.

[Enter DIONYSUS and JAMES.]

JAMES: Simone Du Buvoir says
that men want their partners to yield to
their every demand
whilst keeping their autonomy.
A juggling act in juxtaposition.
That is to say: men want the chase,
and they want to win,
over and over again.
Well, I have shown that I know how to
play the game
to elicit desire,
and yet it is not enough.
If I do not control or manipulate,
they all think I am simple:
if I do manipulate, they think I am evil.

DIONYSUS: None of them understand the brilliant
game you play,
nor the trap you are stuck in.
Chin up.
You wield the *Gleichnis*.
Anything else
and you will have wasted your time
on an idiot that believes you the idiot.

JAMES: It can't be so.
With all his riches and his success?
He must know the game better than I.

DIONYSUS: It is so.

He told you himself he does not play
games.
He is merely an idiot.

JAMES: It can't be so…

DIONYSUS: Strength is not in stifling emotions
but in channeling them.
Victory and failure are only cycles,
an ebb and flow of action and reaction.
I have no qualms telling your story
for the only shameful thing about it
is the way you have
been treated.
Men in ages past have killed for much
less.
This country offers you no role models,
and if you could not find a positive
mentor,
the least you could find was the most
selfish, carnivorous man
possible
and slipstream in his trail of
destruction—
since it is all other men that abide him.
But pushed from his slipstream,
the beast is of no further benefit:
cut him loose and announce yourself.
Stockholm and Orange have fallen
to Antinous
who cannot be raped.
Where next?

JAMES: But first... will they understand me?
Am I too cryptic? Too poetic?

DIONYSUS: Beautiful boy,
they do not understand
because they choose not to understand.
You have done all you can.
You cannot make them listen.
You have cried most bravely—
a war-cry.
Dionysus does not plead.

JAMES: And if they come to punish us?

DIONYSUS: Ha! Let them try.
We are the wilderness.
If they smother us,
they only smother themselves.
Let us go and drink and dance!
The Bacchanalia begins again.

[Exit DIONYSUS and JAMES].

Thank you to my parents who always loved me unconditionally and did the best they could.

To my sister who is lovely and kind, despite the moments I have written about.

To David who found me at my lowest and gave me the stability not just to survive but to thrive.

To Antonio, my brother, my voyager.

To Josh who I owe a lot of dancing.

To Chuck who puts up with me.

To Peter who let me in.

To John M. who told me I was a writer.

To John H., my philosophical guide and mentor.

To Margaret who showed me what literature could be.

To Douglas who recognises light and beauty better than anyone.

To Jean Genet and Veronica Franco for their bravery.

To my many friends over the different periods of my life who kept me going.

And to my piggy who is almost more man than I know what to do with. Almost.

About the Author

James Michael Tolcher was born in Brisbane, Australia. He has a Bachelor of Arts in Writing and English Literature from the University of Queensland. His experience is largely in being a boytoy for rich and powerful men, which would have been a lot more fun if men weren't the absolute worst. He's not particularly scared of them though, so he wrote this book.

Milton Keynes UK
Ingram Content Group UK Ltd.
UKHW010646031023
429856UK00004B/176